Your School's Child-Centered Summer Program

Your School's Child-Centered Summer Program

Independent School Management, Inc.
1316 N. Union Street, Wilmington, DE 19806

All rights reserved. No part of this book may be reproduced or transmitted in any form or by any means, electronic or mechanical, including photocopying, scanning, recording, or by any information storage and retrieval system without the permission of Independent School Management, except for brief quotations with attribution.

Disclaimer: Independent School Management, Inc. (ISM) provides management consulting services to private schools. ISM is not a law firm. No service or information provided by ISM should be construed as legal advice. All web links and references in this book are correct as of the publication date, but may have become inactive or otherwise modified since that time.

Copyright © 2018 by Independent School Management, Inc.

Printed in the United States of America

ISBN-13: 978-1-883627-18-8

Contents

Introduction 5

The Benefits of Your Summer Program 7

Your Role as the Summer Program Director 11

Getting Started: Defining and Planning Your Summer Program 23

Hiring and Training Teachers and Staff 37

Summer Program: Year-Round Schooling and the Third 'Semester' ... 53

Child Safety and Risk Management 67

Handling Monetary Issues 73

Marketing and Promotion 83

Summer Program as a Recruitment Strategy 97

Assessing Your Program and Preparing for Next Year 103

Conclusion 113

Introduction

As Summer Program Director, you likely realize that a summer program provides a valuable educational opportunity for children, as well as many other benefits. Parents of your current students appreciate having the program available for their children and see it as a valuable service.

A summer program is an excellent source of auxiliary income that lets your school extend its mission beyond the school year and to a greater number of students. It is a wonderful recruiting conduit as well, introducing your school to potential students and giving them a "taste" of what your school offers.

The book you hold in your hands is based on the experience of the Consultants of Independent School Management and:

- their consulting in private schools for more than four decades;
- articles published in ISM's management advisory letter *Ideas & Perspectives*, and
- materials used for teaching in ISM's various workshops and seminars.

Throughout this book, we use a fictional, K–12, coed day school, I&P Academy, to provide examples and samples to better explain the strategies and techniques discussed. These are intentionally generic in nature so you can easily adapt them for your school's unique character and mission.

The Benefits of Your Summer Program

"I have a conviction that a few weeks spent in a well-organized summer camp may be of more value educationally than a whole year of formal schoolwork."

Charles Eliot, former President of Harvard University, in his 1922 treatise on education

Private schools always strive to be of service to their current families and their children, improve the school's financial position, and recruit new students. One way to meet your school's goals is to institute a summer program. No other operation would allow its otherwise productive facilities to sit idle for one-third of the year, so why should your school? Building maintenance, grounds work, insurance, salaries, and utilities are all 12-month expenses that need not be borne solely by school-year tuition and fundraising.

When your school offers a quality summer program, it generates various benefits—during the summer and all year long.

- A summer program provides a **valued service to current parents** looking for summer care for their children. Families that use your school's extended care program during the school year need the same option during the summer. When you meet parents' needs, you strengthen their bond with your school. With more dual-working parents, and more parents demanding diverse and specialty programs, planning your summer program must address their concerns and needs. When they know they can rely on your quality and their children feel comfortable and secure with you, why go elsewhere?

- Families not currently involved with your school may also need the services your summer program provides, which creates **new and valuable recruitment opportunities**. When your summer program is open to the community, it attracts prospective families to your campus. An enjoyable summer experience and the opportunity to get to know your teachers and campus may lead parents and students to investigate what you have to offer during the school year. Follow up with these families. Make sure they receive a copy of your viewbook and know how to apply. You might even hold an open house specifically for them.

- Your program can provide **summer employment for your school's teachers**. For private schools that struggle to pay their teachers a competitive wage, summer supplements can be a telling benefit and can contribute to your ability to hold onto good teachers. Summer program can also be a valuable tool for recruiting and re-recruiting faculty. When they can supplement their income by working in the summer program, it's another good reason to choose your school—and stay.

- Your summer program can provide **leadership training opportunities** for potential administrators on your staff.

- From an academic perspective, your program may also provide opportunities to **create and test new, innovative programs.** This is less likely to occur during the regular school year. Teachers can create classes built around their interests and hobbies. They can then share their enthusiasm with young people (one of the primary reasons they first chose to teach). Or they can go into their subject area in more depth, developing classes that go beyond what they can fit into the curriculum during the school year.

- You can offer a **service to students who need remediation or seek acceleration**, besides providing them with an enriching experience as they explore interests and develop talents and skills. Also, students you admit on academic probation can have their academic weaknesses addressed based on your program rather than someone else's.

- Your summer program can be a major component in **12-month facility usage**. The only drawback may be that you are trying to carry out your summer program, major maintenance, and renovation projects simultaneously. But, with careful scheduling, you can set aside those areas that need attention and devote the rest of your campus to summer activities.

- Adding this program creates another **income stream to supplement tuition and fees**. Unlike donated money, this is hard income the school can "count on" receiving.

- A strong summer program can **enhance the school's image** as motivated students spread positive word-of-mouth, improving your relationship with your community.

A national research project on summer camp outcomes, involving more than 5,000 campers and their parents, was conducted by Philliber Research Associates and the American Camp Association during the summers of 2002 and 2003. The survey findings indicated the campers had significant, positive outcomes in four major areas: (1) positive identity, (2) social skills, (3) physical and thinking skills, and (4) positive values and spirituality. Apart from the substantial benefits of a summer program to your school, always keep in mind the perhaps greater benefits to your program's students. A strong, well-organized summer program curriculum, with various student-centered activities, can have an incredible impact on children throughout the year.

There is also research, going back to the 1970s, indicating that being out of school during the summer leads to losses in achievement, creating an academic drop over those months. Learning rates decrease. On the other hand, research shows that you can counter this academic drop by providing educational experiences for children in summer programs. For example, reading comprehension and vocabulary test scores are typically higher for students who participate in summer reading programs than those who do not. If your summer program provides various avenues for learning—e.g., remedial and advanced academics, adventure offerings, tutoring, technology classes, performing and fine arts—your students are better prepared for the following school year.

Your Role as the Summer Program Director

The summer program has changed dramatically in most private schools over the years. It's no longer a small-scale operation designed as a service for school families, offering a handful of arts-and-crafts classes and outdoor activities. It's actually a year-round (not a three-month) business, one that can have a significant impact on recruitment, re-recruitment, and the bottom line. A successful program brings in students from the wider community, bonds current students over the summer months, reinforces the school's image, and generates auxiliary income.

The Summer Program Director works throughout the school year to plan classes, set the schedule, allocate facilities, hire staff, identify equipment, purchase materials, deal with finances, and handle internal and external marketing. In essence, this position is an administrative one, operating a smaller-scale but parallel school over the summer months. The Director is responsible for nearly all the same functions overseen by the School Head.

The Summer Program Director is an administrator who already serves on the Leadership Team. You should get input on decisions and integration with other areas of school operations needed to support the program. As Summer Program Director, you should attend, as appropriate, administrative planning meetings and Leadership Team meetings, and contribute to developing the school's strategic plan. Everyone benefits from the increased interaction and communication, and the administrative staff gains a clearer picture of the summer program's operations, challenges, and the benefits it brings to the school and its families.

Involvement in administrative meetings also clarifies the Summer Program Director's position. If you already work for the school, you may end up supervising colleagues (e.g., you, as a middle school teacher, manage the summer program, and the Middle School Head teaches a summer class). Sometimes you may even be your own "boss." The shift in roles can be a difficult one.

Before defining your program, you must first determine your own expectations and goals as the Summer Program Director at your particular school. Take time to reflect on your past season(s)—or, if this is your first time in the position, reflect on experiences you have had that prepare you for this moment in your career.

Self-Knowledge Inventory

Take a moment to assess yourself on the following dimensions, circling your response on a scale of 1–9 (9 being high and 1 being low). This is not meant to be evaluative, but merely to help you gain personal perspective. Be honest with yourself, otherwise the exercise won't be helpful.

Determining Your Self-Knowledge Level

1. I understand the business of the summer program completely (finances and budget).

    1   2   3   4   5   6   7   8   9

2. I understand the operations of the summer program completely (facilities, janitorial, food service, transportation).

    1   2   3   4   5   6   7   8   9

3. I understand the advancement of the summer program completely (marketing).

    1   2   3   4   5   6   7   8   9

4. I understand the academics of the summer program completely (program offerings).

    1   2   3   4   5   6   7   8   9

5. I am an excellent planner and create the necessary systems to support my plans (including data collection and management).

    1   2   3   4   5   6   7   8   9

6. I am comfortable with adults and thoroughly enjoy working with them.

    1   2   3   4   5   6   7   8   9

7. I understand and apply the principles of time management, maintaining a healthy balance in my personal and professional life.

    1   2   3   4   5   6   7   8   9

8. I am action-oriented, persevering, and focused on results.

    1   2   3   4   5   6   7   8   9

9. I am highly ethical, always working with integrity.

    1   2   3   4   5   6   7   8   9

10. I am highly supportive of my faculty and staff.

    1   2   3   4   5   6   7   8   9

11. I am highly supportive of my students.

    1   2   3   4   5   6   7   8   9

12. I am highly supportive of parents.

    1   2   3   4   5   6   7   8   9

13. I have an inspired and inspirational commitment to the summer program mission.

    1   2   3   4   5   6   7   8   9

14. I give public, positive reinforcement to deserving employees in all categories.

      1   2   3   4   5   6   7   8   9

15. I am highly predictable in my responses to events, both "good" and "bad."

      1   2   3   4   5   6   7   8   9

16. I communicate clearly and I listen accurately.

      1   2   3   4   5   6   7   8   9

Personal and Professional Development: Identify the top item that you would like to improve. It may or may not be your lowest score. Choose the item that would have the most impact for your job this year.

Primary Item for Improvement: _____

_____
_____
_____

Communication and Integration

The exchange of information is particularly important in the following areas.

Admission and marketing. When the leaders of the summer program, admission, and marketing functions work closely together, the summer program can generate applications and boost the school's image.

- As the Summer Program Director, involve yourself to some degree in developing the school's marketing plan. The summer program should have its own internal and external efforts, which need to be coordinated with the school's overall plan regarding timing, message, and image.
- Advertising, direct mail, and social media used to promote the summer program, when done effectively, add to the perception of the school's overall quality.
- The summer program attracts students from other schools in the community, bringing them to your campus and involving them with your students and teachers. How will you follow up with these prospects?

- A successful summer program produces good word-of-mouth about your school—a significant recruiting tool, as well as further validation for current parents that they have made the right choice.
- As a key service and a primary generator of auxiliary income, include the summer program in the school's viewbook, website, and annual report.

Finances. If you have little experience with finance, you'll need to work closely with the Business Manager in developing and monitoring the program's budget. Explore strategies to maximize revenue and hold down costs. You may coordinate purchases with Department Chairs, the Athletics Director, and others to share the cost of buying materials that are also used during the academic year (e.g., soccer balls, science equipment, art supplies).

Close communication with the Business Manager facilitates accurate accounting of the program's revenues and expenses. Be sure to include this information in the operating budget.

Facilities. You must coordinate the scheduling and use of classrooms, gyms, and other spaces inside the school, as well as fields and equipment. Program needs must be balanced with other activities on campus over the summer months. The Facilities Manager will carry out maintenance and renovation projects. The Admission Office may conduct summer open houses. The school may also need meeting space, and may rent use of the facilities to outside groups.

Personnel. You see teachers and administrators who teach in the program from a different perspective. In summer offerings, teachers often teach their avocations rather than their "normal" subjects (e.g., the history teacher who offers a photography class). They may try out a section they would like to add to an existing course in the regular curriculum, or work with different age groups.

You, in effect, see the current teachers and those hired specifically for the summer "audition" for possible school-year roles. What skills do they have that would be valuable? Who would be an excellent career day speaker? Who shows creativity and leadership? Whose hobby would make an interesting article for the school newsletter, or even the local newspaper? Which teachers, hired for the summer program, could be candidates for school-year openings?

With the coordination and communication that need to occur between the summer program and various areas of school operation, it makes sense for you to be involved, as appropriate, in planning and administrative sessions. Both the school-year and summer programs benefit.

So, Where Does the Summer Director Fit In?

During the summer, of course, it's clear you'll need considerable back-up. You're working full-time, focusing on day-to-day administrative tasks—in short, reacting to the immediate.

However, during the academic year, the need for administrative support becomes more intermittent. What resources are available as you likely work part-time to plan classes, recruit instructors, promote the program, and prepare for the coming summer's programmatic excellence and financial success?

The Summer Program Director can occupy an awkward place within the overall administrative and employment structures in a school. You might be a Leadership Team-level administrator, another administrator or teacher, the Director of Auxiliary Programs (which would also include before- and after-school activities), or an "outsider" hired specifically to operate the summer program.

During the summer, the Summer Program Director is the CEO of a "satellite" school, a position roughly akin to (but not supplanting) the School Head. The summer program's operation mirrors the academic-year school. Many of the same administrative functions are necessary, and can be performed by present administrators. It needs to be clear to them that they, in effect, "work for" the Summer Program Director.

However, during the academic year, when you work as a fellow administrator or a teacher, the authority level changes. The awkwardness comes when people face shifting gears in the way they interact with one another.

Relationships With Administrators and Others

A summer program can mean extra work for almost every member of the administration. Coordinated by the Summer Program Director, the contributions of each administrator are needed to promote the overall success of the program. All must understand the role they play—that they "work for" you at certain times, and their cooperation, support, and respect are essential. This is especially true when you come to the position with a background in academics and lack experience in other areas of a school's operations—facilities, finances, public relations, and marketing.

Consider how the Summer Program Director interacts with the following five segments of your school. Then take steps during the school year to enhance the support required for an efficient and successful summer program.

- **School Head.** The Head appoints the Summer Program Director and defines the authority level of the position. If the Director is the "Summer CEO," then the Head is essentially your "Board." The Head sets the tone by impressing on the administration the importance of cooperation with the Summer Program Director. Accomplish this by:

    – reinforcing the authority delegated to you;

    – educating all constituencies (including the Board) about the value of the summer program to the school (financial, recruiting, image, faculty summer employment, etc.);

    – providing time on Leadership Team and faculty meeting agendas for summer program reports; and

    – serving as a court of last resort in those rare instances when necessary.

- **Business Office.** Next to the Head's support, cooperation of the Business Manager is most vital. During the academic year, the Business Manager can help you devise and finalize the summer program budget. Assistance can also be given in arranging contracts for summer program employees or outside service providers, and making sure the school and its summer program employees have adequate insurance coverage. This last item can be important since summer programs typically offer a greater number of physical activities and frequent off-campus trips.

    Within the Business Office, the bookkeeper can help with the accounting chores, during the academic year and the summer. Bookkeeping assistance is valuable at registration time and the beginning of each session.

    Either the Business Manager or the bookkeeper can help you create and manage a budget-tracking program that is compatible with the Business Office's accounting software. With this program, you'll have day-to-day oversight of the program's budget and be able to provide the Business Office with the financial information required to track the program as part of the school's overall budget.

- **Facilities.** The Summer Program Director must collaborate with the Facilities Manager. The two of you carefully coordinate facility, field, and playground use. While the summer program makes extensive use of the school's plant, this is also the time of year when repairs, renovation, adaptations, and detailed cleaning occur. In addition, the summer program has its own daily maintenance and custodial needs.

- **Advancement (Development, Admission, Marketing Communications)**

    1. The Summer Program Director and the Admission Director must have a symbiotic relationship. They should share databases, with each pursuing leads developed by the other. Inform students admitted for the coming year about the summer program. In addition, you can supervise any new students whose admission or placement is dependent on successful completion of work in the school's summer program.

    2. While development personnel may be called on to provide little direct support (except when it is responsible for marketing), you can assist in the development effort. Solicit all nonschool summer program families for special donations to fund enhancements that directly benefit the summer program and, therefore, their children. Keep in mind that all funds raised must go through the Development Office.

    3. Publications and communication personnel can assist you with marketing and advertising, internal and external.

- **Division Directors.** Division Directors can help in many areas. They can identify and help recruit teachers, advisers, and junior counselors—from inside and outside the school. If there is an academic credit component, they can supervise instruction and curriculum and evaluate faculty members. The Division Director can also use the summer program (with your cooperation) as a way to train and orient new teachers or to let returning faculty members "try out" a special-interest course.

- **Teachers.** Since the ultimate success of any summer program is directly related to the quality of the teachers, the school's faculty can provide stimulating and captivating offerings that attract and hold students. However, faculty members need to understand the unusual authority of the Summer Program Director. You may be their academic-year colleague, but still must have the responsibility to accept or decline a proposed summer offering. Act as their supervisor in all summer program matters, regardless of the time of the year.

The Summer Program Director must arrange for internal administrative support for the program. Clerical support is necessary, with increased efforts during registration time in the spring. During the summer, an administrative assistant should handle the day-to-day office tasks, freeing you to supervise the program, visit classrooms, and "put out fires." Also, you need to appoint a second-in-command empowered to act in your absence.

Because the summer program's administrative requirements mirror those of the school during the academic year, administrators and others need to understand what is expected of them in support of the program. This requires tactful collaboration by all concerned, with the overt support of the School Head.

Consider the following example of a typical Summer Program Director's annual time line. The responsibilities are considerable.

Summer Program Director Time Line

	June	July	Aug	Sept	Oct	Nov	Dec	Jan	Feb	Mar	Apr	May
Design Program												
• Research		▬▬▬▬▬▬▬▬▬▬▬▬▬▬▬										
Create Program												
• Calendar				▬▬▬▬▬▬▬▬								
• Courses			▬▬▬▬▬▬▬▬▬▬▬▬▬									
• Schedule							▬▬▬▬▬▬▬▬					
Staffing												
• Coordinators			▬▬▬▬									
• Teachers			▬▬▬▬▬▬▬▬▬▬▬▬▬▬▬▬▬									
• Salaries/Policy			▬▬▬▬▬▬▬▬▬▬▬									
• Evaluation	▬▬▬▬▬▬▬▬▬▬▬▬											
Marketing												
• Brochure/Flyer						▬▬▬▬▬▬▬▬▬▬						
• Inform												
— Faculty				▬▬▬▬▬▬▬								
— Parent Org.							▬▬▬▬▬▬▬▬▬▬▬▬▬▬▬▬▬▬▬▬▬▬▬▬▬					
• Communities								▬▬▬▬▬▬▬▬▬▬▬▬▬▬▬▬▬▬▬				
• Promotion	▬▬▬											
Finance												
• Budget						▬▬▬▬▬▬▬▬▬▬▬▬▬▬▬						
• Tracking	▬▬▬											
• Overhead						▬▬▬▬▬▬▬▬▬▬▬▬▬▬▬▬▬▬▬▬▬▬▬▬▬▬▬▬▬▬▬▬▬▬▬▬▬						
Facilities												
• Plant Set-up									▬▬▬▬▬▬▬▬▬▬▬▬▬▬▬▬			
— Coordinate										▬▬▬▬▬▬▬▬▬▬▬▬		
— Custodial	▬▬											▬▬▬
Admission												
• Inquiries	▬▬▬▬▬▬						▬▬▬▬▬▬▬▬▬▬▬▬▬▬▬▬▬▬▬▬▬					
• Keep records	▬▬▬▬▬▬							▬▬▬▬▬▬▬▬▬▬▬▬▬▬▬▬▬				
• Statistics	▬▬▬▬▬▬▬▬▬▬▬▬▬▬											
Program												
• Opening	▬▬											▬
• Evaluation	▬▬▬▬▬											

The Summer Program Director's Compensation

Compensation for the Summer Program Director has few "rules" attached to it in a school's general practices. By understanding the nature of your administrative role and placing an appropriate value on it, your school positions the program as an integrated part of mission delivery that benefits the school in multiple ways.

Consider the responsibilities of your position. They are significant, including:

- directing a school-sanctioned program;
- developing a vision for the program and executing it;
- evaluating and approving courses;
- evaluating, hiring, and supervising teachers and coaches;
- operating a budget;
- being responsible for risk management of the program;
- marketing the program and recruiting participants, usually from within and outside the school;
- communicating with parents; and
- providing onboarding for new teachers and coaches, to ensure outside hires are knowledgeable about your school's mission and in accord with it, and to train student leaders in programs such as counselors-in-training.

Clearly this is a CEO-type position with a supervisory role, requiring management and leadership skills, and considerable technical skills. Don't consider this merely as an add-on position with marginal connection to the school.

When discussing compensation with the School Head and Business Manager, the following questions may be helpful in detailing the implications of this position.

1. **To whom do you report?** In ISM's experience, most Summer Program Directors report directly to the School Head. This implies they have the same responsibilities as any Leadership Team member. Even where you report to a position such as the Assistant School Head, the Upper School Director, the Athletic Director, or the Business Manager, it still represents a position higher than that of faculty.

2. **Where does this compensation sit in the budget?** Do not consider this as dollars requiring an income offset. If the school sanctions this is as a school program, the compensation is a school operating expense. All other expenses can and should be set against income.

3. **How is this compensation benchmarked internally?** Given that this is an administrative position with great responsibilities, the benchmark for compensation should be within the school's administrative levels. You supervise, administer, plan, organize, and you're an important image-maker for the school. Your compensation should reflect those administrative duties.

4. **What percentage of your time is allotted to this position during the school year (the planning period) as well as in the summer (the full-time period)?** This is clearly not an hourly position. During the program, the Summer Program Director often works long days, arrives early to open and ensure everything is operating well, and leaves after the final walk-around to check teaching areas.

Irrespective of the size of the program, your school should benchmark compensation against a level of administration compensation negotiated between you, the School Head, and the Business Manager.

Getting Started: Defining and Planning Your Summer Program

Before defining your program, you must first determine your own expectations and goals as the Summer Program Director at your particular school. Take time to reflect on your past season(s)—or, if this is your first time in the position, reflect on those experiences that you have had that prepare you for this moment in your career.

Create Your Summer Program Mission Statement

In No. 13 in the "Determining Your Self-Knowledge Level" on page 12, we alluded to the summer program mission. A targeted, succinct mission is the key to differentiating your summer program from competing programs. When creating (or rewriting) your mission statement, first consider your school's mission statement and how your program parallels it. Note also the ideal characteristics of a mission statement are that it:

– be memorable (value-laden);

– be marketable (differentiates and distinguishes); and

– answer the core question: Why does this program exist (essential purpose)?

With this in mind, use the following form to develop your mission statement.

Developing Your Summer Program Mission Statement

What is my school's mission statement? _____
_____
_____
_____

Why do we want a summer program? _____
_____
_____
_____

What values will children learn in our program? _____
_____
_____
_____

Which children will benefit from our program? _____
_____
_____
_____

What distinguishes our program from the competitors? _____
_____
_____
_____

DRAFT MISSION STATEMENT _____
_____
_____

FINAL MISSION STATEMENT _____
_____
_____

Examples of Summer Program Mission Statements

- The mission of our summer program is to provide an opportunity for personal growth, increased self-esteem, and friendship building. We hope to create a space for young people to learn how to work as a group while gaining confidence in their unique abilities as individuals.

- Our mission is to enrich the spiritual, emotional, physical, and social life of each camper in a safe and happy environment. We strive to help campers experience day-to-day Christian living emphasizing character, commitment, caring, respect, friendship, and generosity.

- Our summer program is committed to attracting and educating qualified students from diverse backgrounds. We provide students an academic enrichment experience and the opportunity to live independently in a residential community among students from throughout the United States and the world.

Design a Benefit-Oriented Summer Program

You've determined your summer program mission statement, your prospective students, and your prospective faculty members. Summer programs should be rich with opportunities for students, but also as convenient and flexible as possible for parents. Now, before designing your program, consider your essential responsibilities as the Summer Program Director, including:

- evaluating program offerings, staff, equipment, and facilities;
- checking what your competition offers and looking for programs not available in your area that you can provide;
- reviewing the calendar for the program and placing major events on the school master calendar;
- seeking input from your staff on your strengths and weaknesses as Summer Program Director, then reviewing your own performance;
- reviewing the flow of data between your office and the Admission Office;
- critiquing your brochure, advertisements, and other marketing efforts (especially your school's website and social media);
- meeting with the Facilities Manager to review the summer schedule and begin looking forward to next year;
- collecting comments, informally or through a survey or comment cards, from participating parents, students, and staff members; and
- generating statistics to allow year-to-year comparisons. Take a close look at participation levels and your program's final budget figures.

Based on your assessment, start developing your plans. You typically have only a few months to determine next summer's offerings, hire personnel, and develop your marketing strategies.

Determine Your Goals

As part of the goal-setting process, consider whether you need to:

- expand the number of classes and activities you offer;
- replace some outdated offerings with fresh, new ones;
- boost participation levels;
- meet parents' requests for expanded hours;
- increase your program's length;
- produce more income; and
- improve skills—the staff's and your own—by sending personnel to a course or workshop.

Your school's current grade levels and facilities do not have to define the features of your program. For example, your school may serve middle and upper division students during the school year. But there's no reason you can't offer suitable summer activities for younger children, as long as space is available and the demand exists.

If you lack extensive facilities or find there's a strong demand for a program your campus can't support, look beyond your site. What do local schools, churches, and recreational programs have available? Perhaps you can transport students to the YMCA for swimming lessons or to a nearby riding academy for a trip on horseback. (Check with your Business Office to make sure the school's insurance covers such activities and, if not, add a rider to the school's policy.) For preschool through grade 5, target the benefits to the parents; they decide to enroll. Starting with grade 6, shift more focus to the students—they become the decision-makers (with parental approval).

Programs for the Younger Set

Parents of preschool and lower division children, in particular, need a program that coincides with their schedules. Offer a strong benefit by providing a full day of activities (plus extended day) and running your program all summer long—from the end of school to the start of fall classes.

Another primary concern for parents is ensuring the summer program provides a "safe haven," a place where their children are protected and feel comfortable.

These parents also want more from a summer program than baby-sitting and macaroni-and-glue crafts. They focus on value for their dollar, and they seek a quality experience with a strong learning component.

They will favor your program if you offer their children opportunities to:

- strengthen or enhance academic skills;
- develop a talent through art, drama, music, dance, etc.;
- compete and improve skills through sports programs;
- take field trips to historic and cultural sites;
- engage in traditional summer camp activities; and
- (unstated but essential) have fun and make friends.

As you plan a program for these age levels, consider offering various options each day, in 60- or 90-minute blocks. (The daily schedule might look like the one in the accompanying table.)

In putting your calendar together, consider dividing the summer into one- or two-week modules. This approach allows parents to sign up for the times that fit their schedule and skip a module as needed to take a family vacation.

As a way of communicating the benefits of your program to parents, plan to hold a short demonstration of the skills learned at the end of each module. The children might perform a play, carry out a science experiment, or jump into the pool to show their mastery of the frog kick.

Expanded Opportunities for Older Students

For middle and upper school students, a successful program must offer the benefit of adultlike activities and a wider range of choices. College-bound students are attracted to a combination of summer fun and academically oriented courses. To appeal to these students' growing maturity, offer various options, less-structured time for socializing, and classes that provide an in-depth concentration on life skills. Opportunities to perform "on their own" (for example, in athletics and on stage) are attractive to this age group.

Middle school students look for:

- meaningful community service projects;
- opportunities to help younger students, as tutors and counselors-in-training;

- computer skill-building in database management, graphic design, website creation;
- sports activities at all levels, basic to advanced, including such "exotic" offerings as fencing, martial arts, and horseback riding;
- group activities that involve skills and socialization;
- projects and experiments;
- visual and performing arts;
- creative writing; and
- study skills.

Programs designed for upper division students should offer various options throughout the day. Students in this age group select courses and activities as they would at college. They seek courses that allow them to:

- accelerate in a subject;
- learn a skill that translates into success in college or the working world;
- acquire greater skill in an activity or sport; or
- move into the "adult" world.

They see benefits in:

- advanced academic courses;
- SAT preparation courses;
- practice in writing the college admission essay;
- debate team training;
- studio art classes;
- drama workshops, especially those that culminate in a performance;
- personal growth experiences such as travel, meaningful social-justice work, and counseling;
- computer skill-building;
- driver's education; and
- various sports, particularly involving elite training or competition.

Take the time now to evaluate your summer program from a benefit-oriented perspective, to increase its value and success level.

I&P Academy Summer Sessions **(Sample Daily Schedule, Preschool and Lower Divisions)**	
7:30–8:30	Breakfast or snack Free play and socialization
8:30–9:30	Academic skills block: reading skill development; math, history, science discovery
9:30–9:45	Snack
9:45–11:30	Arts block: visual and performing arts
11:30–12:00	Lunch Quiet time: nap or story time for youngsters
12:00–1:00	Free choice of pottery, computer, drawing, painting for older children
1:00–2:30	Camp activities block: games, sports, swimming
2:30–4:00	Special project block: field trip, nature hike, group activity
4:00–5:00	Concluding activities: play, quiet time
5:00–6:00	Extended day: scouting programs, music and art lessons, outdoor activities

Possible Courses

"The same old classes again this year!" That's the last comment you want parents and kids to make when they open your summer program brochure. Still, you know you need a balance between those successful standbys and the new offerings. With too many unfamiliar courses, you run the risk of lowering enrollment. You may also want to keep it simple and avoid classes that get into a lot of preparation, equipment, or space, or require special skills of the instructor.

So how do you come up with strong new courses that are fun, attention-grabbing, and easy to implement? Summer Program Directors and staff members in private schools across the country have put their creativity to work and developed low-maintenance classes with high kid appeal. Wondering what courses and content to provide in your summer program? Use your imagination—but keep in mind the needs of your participants and the mission. Always remember to make it FUN!

Here are some suggestions, just to prime the pump.

- Create a Concoction: Be a mad scientist in a well-stocked lab. Here you can teach basic chemistry, using simple, hands-on experiments.
- Get Out of Town: Ropes course, canoeing, and an overnight camping and hiking trip.
- What's With the Web?: Instruct students on webpage design and the proper use of social media.
- Europe in Five Days: Explore five European cities through traditions, sights, food, and music.
- Mind Over Matter: Opportunities to explore mathematical concepts for real-life problems.
- Mexican Tales: Participate in telling Aztec and Mayan myths. Make jewelry, mold pottery, and create elaborate headdresses.
- Just Desserts: Prepare various dessert favorites from start to finish. Class cookbook included.
- Art to Wear: Create your own designs and paint T-shirts and other apparel.
- A Star Is Born: Join in creating a script, developing props and scenery, and designing costumes.
- International Camp: Learn about other cultures through arts and crafts, cooking, music, literature, and storytelling. (Two-week blocks with a culminating performance.)
- Build a City: Learn about the important parts of a city and its people.
- Gears and Gizmos Workshop: Join us for the ever-popular exploration of "what makes things work."
- It's a Mystery: Can you compete with Sherlock Holmes? Solve the mystery of the week!
- Science in the Kitchen: Learn about how the best cooking incorporates science.
- Movies and History: Explore popular films and their place in history. After watching each film, students discuss it in its historical context.
- Come Fly With Me: Design and build different flying machines.
- Exploring Chinese Culture: This hands-on class offers kids an opportunity to learn about Chinese culture while creating Chinese crafts and keepsakes.

- Imagination Station: Make puppets and put on exciting shows about your favorite stories and fairy tales.
- Read Between the Lines: Boost phonic skills and increase reading readiness.
- Medieval Times: Travel back in history to the times of knights in shining armor.
- English for Athletes: Introduce students to better writing by having them reflect on their personal moments in sports.
- Sea Safari: Young campers delve into the mysteries of the sea, learning about the animals that live in our surrounding waters.
- Helping Hands: Involve kids in their community through environmental awareness, pollution prevention, recycling, and work with charitable organizations and projects.
- Einstein's Challenge: Learn how to "think differently." You'll be challenged every day with brain-boggling puzzles, games, and mind teasers.

Of course, tap into any local areas and events that might contribute to your program. A day trip to a nearby museum can be instructive and fun, for example. A free concert at the local university? A trip to the public library during an author's book signing? Perhaps there is a public pond in your vicinity—what better opportunity to explore local flora and fauna? Consider all your options. You may be surprised at the variety of potential courses already within reach.

Facilities

A major consideration when planning your summer program is your access to available facilities. How much of the school—indoors and outdoors—will your summer program require? Much depends on your courses offered and the corresponding schedule.

Use the following form to help you focus on your facility needs for the summer program over its weeks of operation. This may reveal overlaps in your schedule, critical costs, and unfulfilled equipment needs.

Facilities Checklist

Complete the catalog of facilities and equipment to be used in this year's summer program.

Room/Building	Equipment	Time of Day	Dates

Summer Program Task Descriptions

As you plan and orchestrate the different aspects of your summer program, consider the following list of general responsibilities. It may seem overwhelming, but please note the elements of the list involve coordination with various members of the Leadership Team. Keep in mind, running a summer program is a team effort—and you're the captain!

Planning: Report to the School Head

- program offerings
  - continuing
  - new
  - discontinuing
- evaluation

- size of program
- timing and calendar
  - modular
  - daily schedule
  - dates
- services
  - food
  - transportation
  - extended day

Personnel: Coordinate With HR Office

- determine people and skills needed
- hiring
- evaluation
- personnel policies
- salaries and benefits
- "firing"

Marketing: Coordinate With Director of Marketing Communications

- determine benefits of the program
- design and publish brochure
- assess and update website and social media
- sell to parents
- sell to faculty and staff
- sell to students
- sell to community
- design advertising and determine placement
- consider promotional materials (e.g., camp T-shirts, magnets, and water bottles)

Finances: Coordinate with Business Manager

- review previous year's operation

- prepare budget
  - personnel
  - materials purchase
  - marketing and advertising expense
  - equipment purchase
  - insurance
  - overhead
  - general expenses
- determine where the net revenue goes (float for the next year, endowment, faculty development, curriculum development, materials and equipment, general revenues)

Maintenance and Facilities: Coordinate With Facilities Manager (or Business Manager)

- create a calendar
- establish procedures and expectations
- coordinate with Plant Manager
- identify custodial arrangements and costs
- set up regular meetings

Personnel: Coordinate With Admission Director

- determine registration process
  - paper
  - online
  - payment options (cash, check, credit card)
- determine standards for admission (as needed and as related to individual courses)
- respond to inquiries
- send follow-up letters
- file applications

- keep statistics
  - inquiries
  - enrollments
  - repeat "customers"
  - average number of courses taken
  - how they heard about the program
  - which school they attend
  - how many students enrolled as new at your school

General

- schedule special promotions
- plan program opening
- set up orientation of faculty and staff members
- plan celebrations
- be "in charge"

Of course, this checklist is only meant as a guide to help you create your own, one specific to your program and its mission.

Hiring and Training Teachers and Staff

You've now determined much of the content of your summer program. As the Summer Program Director, you know the quality of your staff is crucial to the program's success. Providing unique offerings is not enough. Qualified instructors who can attract students and hold their interest must lead the activities.

A first-rate staff is one of your prime marketing tools, whether your program:

- focuses on various "fun-and-learning" activities (in athletics, arts, etc.);
- offers academic advancement, enrichment, or remediation; or
- includes a combination of these elements.

If your summer program is new, families will enroll their children because your staff promises an exciting, worthwhile experience and adds credibility to your offerings. For an established program, a quality staff brings back participants from previous years, and the good word-of-mouth these instructors generate can expand your program's reach, year after year.

Essential Qualities You Seek

Whether you hire staff members from within your school, outside sources, or both, you're looking for more than demonstrated competence in whatever course(s) they lead and an ability to teach. You're looking for specific personal qualities in these employees as well.

Remember that a summer program is significantly shorter than the academic year program, perhaps 10 weeks as opposed to 36. Also, some staff members may be involved for only a portion of the program—perhaps leading a two-week course.

So, all staff members must be able to develop an instant rapport with the participants. They need to be able to capture the students' interest. These individuals must be "pied pipers"—people who naturally draw students. They need to be enthusiastic, imaginative, creative, and patient leaders; they must enjoy what they are doing and relay their own excitement to their students.

How to Identify Pied Pipers in Your School

For many schools, providing summer employment for the school's personnel is a key reason to start a summer program. However, you can't afford to hire current faculty or staff members who are "only in it for the money." They must meet your criteria.

Talk with the School Head, Division Directors, Academic Dean, and lead teachers, and ask them to identify faculty and staff members who exhibit the qualities you seek. Also check with the disciplinarian as one means of assessing how teachers interact with students.

Get permission from the Head to walk around the school and visit classes. Talk to the teachers. Let them know you are interested in learning more about what goes on in the classrooms and in picking up possible ideas for the summer programs. Ask whether it is okay for you to drop in and observe. In your search for potential recruits, look for those teachers who challenge and interest students and who provide experiential, project-based, and child-oriented activities.

Listen to what students and parents say about teachers, both in the classroom and in other areas of school life. Don't ask direct questions. Just keep your ears open. You want to find out how a teacher deals with students in all situations. Remember, patience is one of the qualities you seek.

Find out if any teachers have hobbies that could enhance summer program offerings (e.g., a history teacher who is an amateur photographer or a physical education teacher who is a trained dancer).

Two caveats: Just because a teacher works for the school during the academic year does not mean that same teacher will make a good summer program leader. The upper school art teacher, no matter how skilled in her discipline, may not interact effectively with a group of 11-year-olds or be able to develop age-appropriate summer projects.

You also want to avoid lame ducks. A teacher or staff member who has not been rehired for the coming school year may have difficulty bringing a pied-piper attitude to the summer's activities. Developing a good relationship with the school's leaders may help you avoid this situation; they can suggest that an employee not be considered without specifying the reason. However, you should also have a written policy that gives the school the power to rescind the summer contract in this situation, should it so choose.

Other Sources

Good staff members can also come from outside the school. Look at the substitute list. Is there someone there who has the qualities you seek? What about new teachers hired for the coming academic year? Does the faculty know of anyone? What about a teacher from another private school? A magnet or feeder school?

Other possible sources of qualified staff members include:

- the art league or institute that offers children's classes;
- the local dance academies, which have instructors known to summer program participants and experienced in working with students;
- the local children's theater or a university drama program, which can provide teachers with acting, directing, and stagecraft abilities;
- the junior orchestra, whose conductor is familiar with appropriate music;
- your school's own after-school care program, if it offers classes taught by professionals from off-campus. These people will know your school and attract participants;
- local alumni, who can bring talents to your program; and
- for athletics, local organizations (e.g., the YMCA, Boys and Girls Clubs) and college and university athletic departments.

Of course, you want to use the same procedures in hiring summer employees as you do with regular school-year personnel, including collecting references and conducting background checks.

Keep in mind that attracting qualified "outside" instructors may have benefits for the academic-year program as well. The summer program experience provides a good trial run. The school has an opportunity to identify potential recruits for full-time faculty or staff positions, and the summer program instructor gets a chance to size up the school as a potential employer.

Getting the Word Out

Besides recruiting your summer program personnel through the newspapers and other publications in which the school routinely advertises academic-year vacancies, consider these options:

- include an announcement on your school's website and in the newsletter;
- advertise in publications that reaches people with the skills you seek. Possibilities include church bulletins, newsletters published by community organizations (the Y, arts groups, etc.), and materials directed to people with specific interests (dance, photography, coaching, etc.);
- post notices in local libraries and organization offices, as well as on online classified ad sites that highlight educational positions; and
- let the placement personnel in the local colleges and universities know about positions available.

Hiring carefully selected, imaginative, and talented staff members strengthens your school's summer program, holds personnel problems to a minimum, and attracts participants—new and returning. These pied pipers are the foundation of the program's success.

Contracts

You've selected the best candidates for your summer program staff. Before you begin the hiring process, develop an employment contract and have it vetted by the school's legal counsel—preferably someone familiar with human resources law in your state. Your contract should specify:

- employee salary;
- employee benefits;
- training week schedule (paid or unpaid?);
- orientation dates and times;
- pay period;

- job-starting time and date;
- preprogram requirements (e.g., staff meetings);
- medical requirements (e.g., physicals);
- any required qualifications (e.g., first aid, lifeguard certification);
- cancellation clause;
- minimum course-load guarantee;
- absentee policy;
- process for dismissal;
- job description; and
- any other details or requirements specific to your program.

What to remember about firing:

- Know your state and federal laws. Make sure you are clear on what qualifies as wrongful dismissal. Discuss this with your school's Human Resources Department.
- Record any incident(s) in written form. Make sure they are confirmed either by a summer program leader or by a second source. Communicate your findings to the person and have him or her acknowledge receipt.
- Don't procrastinate! Nothing can pull your program down faster than your refusal to decide on an employee deemed mission-inappropriate.
- Do not hesitate to fire someone because you feel you will have difficulty finding a replacement. If the person is not doing the job as desired, it is likely the other staff members have been covering for that person's negligence.
- Late replacements often pose the most trouble. Ask your senior staff members to keep an eye on them.
- Ensure every staff member is appropriately evaluated!

Essential Background Checks

To protect your institution and its students and employees, your school must conduct effective background checks of each candidate for employment during your summer program. Otherwise, you are at strong risk of facing a scenario that could prove damaging to your school's finances, student and staff safety, and community reputation.

References Versus Background Verification

A comprehensive screening process incorporates two distinct elements: (1) reference checking and (2) background verification.

The term "reference checking" points to the traditional process of speaking with a small handful of professional or "character" references the candidate provides. These may include former supervisors, colleagues, and community members who can speak to that individual's professional skills and personal character. They provide qualitative information about the candidate, and important data points (as well as résumés and interview results) for assessing the candidate's fit with the position requirements and the program's mission, culture, and values.

As the Summer Program Director and "hiring manager," you are best able to target reference questions to the qualitative information being sought. However, if the process stops here, it is dangerously incomplete. The second element of the screening process involves verification of the facts of a candidate's background and history—from an objective or quantitative perspective. This is usually best handled by the Business Manager (or Human Resources Manager, if the school has one) to limit the risk of potentially discriminatory information leaking into the hiring process.

Before You Begin: Complying With the Law

The federal Fair Credit Reporting Act (FCRA) governs use of background screening reports (such as those listed below) purchased from vendors. This is true even if the school is not checking the candidate's credit report, as these reports are deemed to be "consumer investigative reports" and thus governed by FCRA.

The good news is that the primary element of FCRA is easy to comply with—i.e., having the candidate's signed consent before ordering background reports. Provide two documents to all candidates who are interviewed on-campus: (1) Application for Employment and (2) Background Screening Consent Form. If all interviewed candidates sign the latter form, the school will already have it on file when it needs to check the finalist's background. The school should ask its report vendor for the consent form that it recommends, since required consent language and provisions vary by state.

Types of Records and Reports

With various records and reports available, the school should be careful in selecting only those that provide relevant job-related information.

- Criminal history: Conduct this for all employees, for safety purposes.
- Driving record: Order this report for all employees for whom driving on school business (even if just occasionally) is a possibility.
- Education: The school may purchase a report verifying the candidate's educational credentials, or it may simply require the applicant to provide a photocopy of degrees and certificates.
- Employment: The school may buy a report verifying the dates and positions of prior employment or may confirm this information on its own by calling prior employers.
- Credit: Order this report only with significant caution, as the causal relationship between an individual's personal credit history and his or her ability to perform the job is questionable. Rather, the school may choose to focus its efforts on a more thorough criminal screening (e.g., to identify instances of embezzlement or other financial crimes that are much more directly job-related).

Balancing Short-Term Costs Versus Long-Term Risks

Schools must consider the cost and benefit involved when determining "how far back" or "how far and wide" to check. Of course, the more information you ask to have checked, the more costly the report.

Contrast this with the fact the more extensive the report, the more likely it is to safeguard the school from hiring an inappropriate candidate. For example, a standard criminal report from your vendor might check the candidate's criminal history for the past seven years in your state and county. However, if the candidate has lived in several different states during that time period, it may be prudent to order criminal reports and driving records in each state.

If the school currently orders criminal and driving records from a vendor, it is important to know how far back and what locations are covered in the reports. (Depending on state requirements, a school may already be ordering criminal background reports from the FBI, the state's Department of Justice, or other law enforcement agencies. It is equally important to know what locations, types of offenses, and years these reports cover.) Likewise, it is important for schools to know if the report includes checking national criminal databases and the sex offender registry.

Standards: What is 'Forgivable'

The most critical part of the process is establishing a standard for evaluating the information in the background reports when they are received. Take this step now, before the school is involved in considering the case of any particular candidate. With fixed standards in place, administrators have the support they need to make appropriately dispassionate decisions and avoid becoming embroiled in any emotional attachment toward the candidacy of any one individual. This reduces the school's risk for inconsistent or discriminatory treatment of candidates.

Two primary factors influence establishing standards: (1) the mission, culture, and values of the school and (2) the relevance of the transgression to the individual's job. The school can have different standards for different positions if it so chooses, based on the needs of the job.

For example, a DUI conviction 20 years ago during college may be deemed "forgivable" as a "youthful transgression" for those not in driving positions. However, any history of DUI for those in driving-eligible positions is considered unacceptable. The school must establish the general standards in advance.

The following "Background Reports" chart provides samples of reasonable standards. However, it is designed only as a guideline. Each individual school should develop standards appropriate to its mission, culture, and values.

Note that management (specifically, the Head and Business Manager) use these standards when reviewing the results of background screening reports. Do not publish them for employees in general.

Closing the Loop: Communicating Results

The vendor usually delivers the results directly to the Business Manager (or HR person). If the school has established standards, it should not be necessary to communicate anything other than "pass" or "fail" to the hiring manager (Head or Division Head). This protects the candidate and the hiring manager, if you hire the candidate. For example, the manager is at risk if he or she knows potentially discriminatory information about the employee and is alleged to have used this information against the employee during that person's career with the school.

If the information contained in the report disqualifies the candidate, the hiring manager and candidate must be so informed. FCRA requires the school to follow a formal, written, two-step process for notification, to preserve the candidate's FCRA rights, and the candidate can contest any negative information on the report that is in error.

By following the above process, schools can protect themselves, their students, and other employees from the risks that an inappropriate or unsafe hire represents. Plus they comply with all applicable laws.

Sample Background Report Standards

Absent significant mitigating circumstances to the contrary, the following criteria will usually disqualify a candidate from employment with I&P Academy. We base our review of criminal records solely on convictions and do not seek information regarding arrests.*

Report Type	Criteria
Criminal	Any convictions (1) for violent acts, (2) involving fraud or embezzlement, (3) requiring registry as a sex offender, or (4) for untoward acts involving minors.
	Any felony convictions within the past seven years. (Felony convictions longer than seven years ago and misdemeanor convictions will be judged based on the facts of the case.)
Employment	Material misrepresentations about dates of employment, position, title, or duties.
Education	Material misrepresentations about dates of receipt of degree, type of degree, or grades or honors earned.
Motor Vehicle	Three or more moving violations within the past three years (speeding, driving without a license, driving without insurance, etc.).
	Any conviction for DWI, DUI, or similar impairment within the past seven years.

* The school may decide to have the vendor include information on the criminal report pertaining to misdemeanors and felonies (as there are certain misdemeanors that may be problematic for employees in school positions). However, it is vital that it not accept any information about arrests, as this is considered highly discriminatory information.

Counselor-in-Training Programs

Keep in mind that your summer program provides the perfect opportunity to launch a counselor-in-training program. You can bring in your older students as staff members to help maintain your courses and provide role models for your younger students. Such a program can help you:

- develop an excellent pool of future counselors;
- support your leadership program;
- support your community service program;
- create an inexpensive, motivated labor force;
- bring to campus an interesting group of young people with incredible energy;
- increase your return rates among older participants, as they have a specific aim to become a counselor-in-training; and
- establish a training ground for future teachers.

Consider those students in your school who would do well as counselors-in-training—perhaps those who have attended your summer program in the past—and invite them to participate. Pay them as you would for any summer job. Also keep in mind those counselors who have been instrumental in previous summers. They are prime candidates for more training and responsibility in your program.

Use the following form as your guide.

Potential Counselors			
Name	**Grade**	**Name**	**Grade**

Current Counselors for Further Training			
Name	Grade	Name	Grade

Using Outside Contractors for Your Summer Program

When designing programs to meet your school's goals, one of the first decisions to make is management. As the Summer Program Director, should you plan to offer school programs only, offer programs run by outside contractors (and, in essence, lease your facilities to them), or combine these two elements? If you decide to work with contractors, what are the pros and cons?

Outside Contractors

There are many day camps, sports camps or clinics, drama groups, music groups, corporate groups, or programs that serve the economically disadvantaged that would be ready and willing to use your facilities. Most offer a program matching your school's image of excellence, but some may not.

Be sure to call references to assure the quality of personnel and Directors, as well as the contractor's financial standing. Confirm your school's control over the use of the school's name in promotional materials. (Will the program be the I&P Academy Sports Camp run by Coach Doe, or Coach Doe's Sports Camp run at I&P Academy?) Conduct thorough discussions about:

- insurance coverage (the contractor must provide evidence of coverage for review by the school's attorney);
- hiring practices (the contractor must conduct background checks of employees as required by law);
- risk-management procedures for the contractor and for your school; and
- school-contractor coordination.

Then clearly explain these points in a written contract.

The decision to use an outside contractor can only be made after evaluating the advantages and disadvantages for your school's program.

Advantages of an Independent Contractor

Hiring a contractor to handle your summer program may have many benefits.

- The program will be "up and running" in short time—a particular advantage if you are just staring a program or want to offer new options for this summer. All it takes is finding a contractor with a good reputation and negotiating a contract that meets the needs of both parties. (There should be a written contract before any group or person uses your campus, whether the contractor is a member of your school's staff!)
- The school can offer a program without the expenses of an onsite Director, promotional materials, and support staff.
- There are no start-up costs to be borne by the operating budget, and the risk that the program will not "fill" the first summer is reduced. Thus the school is assured a revenue stream based on the terms of the lease arrangement.
- If the program serves the economically disadvantaged, the contractor must raise the funds necessary to run the program and pay the school for the use of facilities and equipment.
- School staff members or graduates hired by the contractor can make a nice summer income. The school assures it meets its goal of providing summer employment for teachers.
- The school can become "connected" with an outstanding organization and gain credibility in the community. This can translate into strong publicity and bring prospective students to campus.

Disadvantages of an Independent Contractor

Hiring an independent contractor to manage your summer program can also have its drawbacks.

- The school must assign a liaison person to work with the contractor. There are many details to work out, primarily concerning:
  - services performed by the school (e.g., cleaning, security, setups of rooms, scheduling mowing when classes or concerts are not in session);
  - school equipment used by the contractor (e.g., athletic equipment from

goals to balls and scrimmage vests; drama costumes, tools, and set materials; computers; art room supplies);
- use of spaces other than the primary space (such as the gym on rainy days, the dining hall for large group meetings, athletic fields); and
- participant conduct (from rules of conduct and use of alcohol for adult groups to maintaining the sanctity and quiet of the administrative offices).

- Financial problems can result if:
    - the school does not set its charge for using the facilities high enough to cover costs and "wear and tear";
    - the fee the contractor charges participants is not high enough to cover the school's lease; or
    - the program does not meet enrollment projections.

The school and the contractor may have to negotiate a settlement, or the school may lose money on the contract. Another alternative, under a multiyear contract, is to reconcile the loss the following year. The school may want to establish a three-year contract that includes an increase each year and can allow for variations. Be careful about one-year agreements unless you are sure that you prefer the control this allows or plan to offer a school-run program next year.

- The school loses control over:
    - hiring employees. They reflect on the school's image whether they work for the school or not; and
    - its facilities in the summer. The contractor will "own" the facilities—and the school personnel assigned to serve the needs of the contractor—during the program.
- The school's image is in the contractor's hands, and will be based on a group's performance over which the school has little control. Parents of children in the contractor's program may transfer their concerns about the program to the school.
- If school staff members become contractors, it may become difficult to bring all programs under the school's direction in the future. If an outside contractor wants to hire a school staff member to run the program at your campus, there can be a conflict over:
    - which entity is the teacher's "employer";
    - which employer gives direction and evaluation;

– which employer pays salaries and benefits (there is a potential for double payment); and

– which employer determines continued employment in the program.

The use of outside contractors can be appealing, and can be highly successful for the school and the contractor. It works! Just be sure your school will not— is not—losing money in the contract and that it meets the goals of the school's summer program. Clear evaluation is required. Use the following template to help focus your thinking.

Program Design: School-Run Versus Third-Party Contractor
Advantages:
1.
2.
3.
4.
Disadvantages:
1.
2.
3.
4.
Combinations (pros and cons):
1.
2.
3.
4.
Director or Coordinator (time, effort, return on investment):
1.
2.
3.
4.

Summer Program Faculty and Staff Manual

Part of training your instructors and staff members is to develop and distribute a manual setting the expectations and parameters of your program. Of course, tailor the manual to your specific summer program. Your manual should cover at least the following elements, and any others that you deem appropriate or necessary.

- Program Mission and Goals
- Personnel Structure and Responsibilities
- Personnel Standards (e.g., standards of conduct, dress code, attendance policy)
- Sexual Harassment Policy
- Security and Safety Procedures (including offsite activities)
- Health Procedures
- Emergency Safety Procedures
- Transportation Standards
- Behavior Management
- Parent Relations Standards

Summer Program: Year-Round Schooling and the Third 'Semester'

As the Summer Program Director, you realize the school's schedule largely dictates your program's schedule. As more schools move toward year-round schooling, your summer program can represent the school's third "semester." This chapter lays out the broad framework for this position, focusing on how this concept affects upper school students, lower and middle school students, and your school's finances and administration.

As mentioned earlier, most schools justify providing a summer program because the program:

- provides fun and mission-appropriate activities for the school's current students;
- drives revenue and provides added income for the school's faculty;
- increases awareness of the school within the community;

- competes with programs established at other schools;
- recruits new students; and
- provides current students with the ability to make up or take academic courses.

None of these are invalidated by year-round schooling. However, clearly the thinking around the summer program must evolve from an activity extrinsic to most school personnel (and not related to the rest of the school year). The job of the Summer Program Director, far from being an extra duty added to the person's "real" job, now has strategic significance.

Schools interested in rethinking how they approach their summer activities should consider the following.

- Do not think of this as an "either-or" situation. Within the year-round schooling context, any or all the justifications above can still be used and extended.
- Keep in mind that moving to year-round schooling carries relatively little risk; it is a transitional process. The first step is to make an attitudinal shift that moves summer program from an extrinsic process to one that is intrinsic to the school's mission and strategic goals.
- Engage the Board of Trustees in this conversation and, in the quadrennial strategic planning process, identify this as the proper and prudent direction for the school.
- Create a plan that identifies steps that will move the school in this direction.
- Engage faculty leaders, team leaders, Department Chairs, and Division Heads in a conversation to understand how you can extend the academic program in a third semester. For schools with a robust academic summer program currently, integrate that program into the curriculum handbook. For schools with no or limited academic components, create steps that encourage summer academic exploration.
- Think about summer experiential education (service learning, trips abroad, research, internships) within the context of the student's ongoing educational process, and provide recognition.
- Create working groups of interested faculty with summer stipends to develop ways to integrate a student's summer experiences into the credit structures of the school.

- Engage the upper school college counselors in a conversation about the impact of a third semester on college application processes.

Treating summer program as a third semester also changes the way in which families come to think about the school. The admission process includes the possibilities of student enrichment that will come through the years spent at the school. Parents are already accustomed to spending considerable amounts in keeping their children occupied over the summer. They understand tuition pays for two semesters, but their children can benefit from a third semester as well.

ISM's position is that year-round schooling is inevitable. Summer program offers a way to think about this as an incremental and understandable progression. Schools currently without summer programs can now plan to offer experiences and courses. Schools without academic components can begin to add those elements to their course catalogs. Schools that already have sophisticated summer programs can further strengthen their programs to even more effectively complement the desired outcomes of the school mission.

Lower and Middle School

In the middle and lower schools, your program slowly transitions to an intentional process that builds on traditional fun and challenge. Those programs of sports, arts, and general and specific interest camps will continue to be a viable model as schools meet the marketplace need for child care during the summer break. More proactive schools might see this move to a "third semester" as an opportunity to challenge their paradigms. There are two changes that impact what schools do—intentionality and innovation.

Intentionality

The current paradigm sees the Summer Program Director take over an almost deserted campus during June, July, and August. Often, many "regular" administrators (except for the Business Manager) head off for a break and professional development, while the Summer Program Director essentially becomes the summer's "School Head."

The intentional approach asks the following two questions.

- In what way does the summer program act as a continuum with your first (S1) and second (S2) semester programs?
- How does a year-round school change your thinking?

The answers differ in various ways. Consider the following suggestions in thinking about this changing paradigm.

1. **If the summer program is a continuum with the rest of the school year, then parts of the semester can act as a programmatic enrichment for students that augments their S1 and S2 experience.** Clearly, you are not going to give up, for example, your moneymaking "Fun in the Sun" camp, even if it has no connection to your mission. You might, however, recognize that alignment between S3 curriculum and S1 and S2 curriculum deepens thinking and allows students to explore learning in a more passionate and consistent way. Because summer programs operate as one- or multiple-week experiences, the chance to go into depth is significant. Local parks and museums that provide Bug Adventures and Solar Sightseeing already recognize this.

Even general interest programs can focus more intentionally on the school's mission and values. Develop activities that promote leadership, peer support, social interaction, sophisticated play, conflict resolution, collaboration, innovation, and creativity. Intentionality increases the perceived value of S3. Its rearticulation as a true part of the school community (despite many students from other places attending) positions the school:

- powerfully in parents' minds;
- deeply in student experience; and
- competitively in the marketplace.

Marketing S3 then becomes less an articulation of a summer program smorgasbord, and more a focus on the school's excellence.

2. **Where your school does not include an upper division, the summer program can offer keynote experiences that make the student better prepared for next-level placement.** This links to a change in the school's thinking and implies a real integration programmatically. Not that a child who does not attend the summer program is disadvantaged, but in that the program is aligned in mission, vision, quality, and values (academic and social-emotional) reflecting the S1 and S2 experience. This is, in truth, an enhancement for students who attend from your own school. They find that S3 improves who they are and what they do. It is equally an attractant for the parent or student from another school who understands what the host school can offer. You thus think about S3 in a strategic way, not just hoping that it goes well and drives some income, but consider it an integral part of the school's life.

Innovation

Moving from school to school provides little indication that any given school has challenged the orthodoxy that leads to typical curriculum. The intentionality of year-round schooling that S3 implies opens opportunity to think out of the box about lower and middle school practices.

First, it treats summer camps, clubs, and courses seriously as part of the program and provokes the question: What barriers are there to having fun like this every day in school?

Semester 3 challenges the idea that:

- students must constantly change from subject to subject to progress academically. Summer camps often do one thing for long periods of time or spend entire weeks exploring one aspect of understanding or action;
- "hurry" is the norm and that rushing means "rigorous." Summer programs tend to be much more relaxed in tempo with plenty of time to think, eat, play, and relax. Yet, by the end of the week, they often have astonishing outcomes (performed plays, rode horses, significantly enhanced sports skills, gained expert knowledge of water and water animals, learned to survive in the woods); and
- more teachers means better teaching. Summer programs often give one teacher to one group of children. They get to know one another almost instantly, form bonds that can last for years, and achieve outcomes that take S1 and S2 teachers months to accomplish.

Second, because it is not (yet) part of the regular curriculum, the summer program offers the opportunity to try new things. When you, as the Summer Program Director, are recognized as an administrator and treated with the same respect and attention, schools can open conversations with the Lower and Middle School Directors, lead teachers, and team leaders. These discussions about pedagogical and programmatic innovation might lead to even greater academic gains than the school currently achieves. Pose the following questions.

- How might S3 help us understand how to personalize for a diverse group of students who all reach the outcome, although in different ways and at different levels?
- How might S3 help us look at play as a valuable medium for learning in S1 and S2?
- In what ways does S3 provide us insights into building curriculum that students love?

- Can we try S1 and S2 approaches in S3 and uncover ways they succeed and fail?
- Why do cross-age groupings work well in S3, and what might that tell us?
- Are there differences in the nature of engagement between S1 and S2, compared with S3?
- Why do kids bond so fast in S3? How does that inform the nature of community?
- How do we make S3 academically challenging while retaining fun? Are those incompatible?

Intentionality and innovation provide academic leaders with two aspects of the same question: How do we improve each student's learning? S3 allows and promotes conversations that can affirm and challenge current practice. Striving toward year-round schooling in a way that enhances quality of learning and life for students and teachers is an enticing and increasingly attractive goal.

Upper School

Consider some key questions from the upper school student's view. The principal objection to the third semester has nothing to do with organization, faculty, money, or facilities. Rather, the main student objection is: I can't imagine doing in the third semester what I've been doing all year. A third "semester" cannot be successful without considering the other two semesters—by the students themselves—as being of high value, entertaining, inspirational, and engaging.

A parent wants the teenager meaningfully engaged over the summer hiatus, in a safe environment, doing something useful. But their motivation to have that school activity is not necessarily strong. The students themselves make the case for the third semester. As the Summer Program Director, consider the following questions.

- Are all of our teachers highly engaging?
- Is student performance universally excellent, including in-class and out-of-class experiences?
- Has the school moved to longer periods of at least 75 minutes?
- Has the school begun to personalize the curriculum, encouraging students to follow their passion and move at their own pace?
- Would you characterize the pace of the first two semesters as frenetic, purposeful, or relaxed?

If you are confident in the quality of your current first two semesters, then it is time to consider other issues, again from the student's view. Let's imagine a question-and-answer session with a group of students the school is attempting to recruit to this new venture.

Question No. 1: Do I get a break?

The year-round calendar has to answer the student's question and show a paced year. The question is valid and, of course, can also be asked by the teacher who is curious about teaching year-round. The following table illustrates this.

	Days	Totals	Comments
Semesters 1 and 2	150	112.5 hours per course	Students typically take six or seven courses of eight available
Semester 3	50	100 hours per course	Less teaching time but more intense teaching time and fewer or no interruptions—three courses available
Weekends	104	52 weeks	All Saturdays and Sundays
Breaks and Holidays	35	7 weeks	Winter, spring, summer breaks, and holidays
Long Weekends	14	7	Four-day weekends
Thanksgiving	3	—	—
School Activities	9	Nonteaching	Homecoming, Field Day, retreats, etc.
Total	**365**	**52 weeks**	**One calendar year**

Under this scenario, students who chose Semester 3 would be at school for 209 out of 365 days.

Question No. 2: What's different about Semester 3?

A selling point of this semester is there would be some significant differences between S3 and the other two.

- There are three courses possible. They might be configured:
  – three every day (two hours a day),

- two a day for 25 days (four hours a day) and an intensive (six to eight hours a day) for 15 days, or
- some other option.

■ Expectations are limited to the course (e.g., no clubs, cocurriculars, student government) and thus no distractions—typically "homework" would be done during the day and evening, and weekends would be free.

■ The teacher is the student adviser, a relationship that ensures an exceptionally high level of personal attention.

Question No. 3: What happens if I get a boring teacher?

This is a great question. Note the caveat to the whole process. Before beginning Semester 3, ruthless selective retention must be practiced. The boring teacher must be evaluated, found to be boring, and not have a contract going forward. However, we would also assume that teachers would be vetted and only excellent teachers engaged. This would, of course, impact the other two semesters, since a standard of excellence is assumed throughout the school year.

Question No. 4: So why should I even consider "giving up" my summer?

There are many excellent reasons to consider enrolling in the third semester.

■ You can satisfy a graduation requirement and make space in the other two semesters for courses that particularly interest you. This may include the arts, doubling up in mathematics or social studies, or taking two world languages.

■ You could take a course to free time for cocurriculars offered during the other two semesters. You could then become involved in varsity athletics or the fall play and spring musical, or maintain your commitments to Model United Nations and student government. You might take a difficult subject that you know requires significant teacher feedback for you to be successful (remember that your teacher is only teaching your class). You may opt to take a class that you can get a B in rather than a C (or A rather than a B) by having less competition for your time.

■ You may be able to take off-site courses, such as:
- science studies doing research in the mountains or at the beach;
- music lessons and going on tour;
- a (credit-worthy) summer production or arts show;
- study of the Civil War that includes visiting key battlefields; or
- an immersion study of a new language.

- You might have been ill at some point in the year and need to repeat a course (maybe not enticing, but practical).
- You are offered courses that would not be possible during the year because of the school's credit requirements that limit innovation.
- Your favorite teacher is offering another course and it would be too much fun to miss.
- You like learning.
- It's something meaningful to do with your summer.
- It's fun.

Question No. 5: Could I still get a job in the summer?

This would depend on how the courses are configured and how many you take. Taking one course only would leave you with plenty of time for a summer job. Taking all three would still leave you with evenings and weekends largely free. So, depending on how S3 is organized and the choices made, there would be time to have a part-time job, see your friends, play sports, and even take a vacation with your family. However, if the courses need evening and weekend work, or are courses that require an immersion experience, clearly the excitement of the course is balanced by the lack of time for other activities.

Semester 3 in upper school is often almost exclusively academic in nature, i.e., enabling the student to truly enrich the course of study, accelerate a program, develop a passion, or make up for lost time. The primary client is the student with the parent acting as supporter in the background. The rationale for making education available to students year-round will not convince all. But it will be attractive to some, maybe many, who consider the opportunity too good to turn down.

This assumes only an internal audience of students, but it would act as an equal attraction to students from other schools. The key here is mutual acceptance of credits by schools in a given geographic area. For some administrators, this might be a difficult concept to accept. In a mutually beneficial collaboration, however, such an acceptance advances the students' and each school's self-interest. If a school refused to collaborate, their best students would naturally be attracted to move to the schools providing such rich opportunities.

Three Administrative Considerations

We have provided examples and insights into Semester 3 as an inevitable expansion of a school's program to year-round.

Now let's look at some administrative considerations for third semester leadership, facilities, and upper school curriculum.

Leadership

The requirement for expert summer leadership implies significant skills and responsibilities. This is an extra "division." However, the leadership options are flexible, which may include (among other possibilities):

- a full-time Academic Administrator in charge of, for example, vertical alignment (curriculum) during the year in a three-division school;
- a full-time Academic Administrator also in charge of an area such as extended care;
- a full-time Summer Program Director who, during the year, has no more than 0.4 FTE teaching responsibilities. (Caveat: This is the least desirable option. It creates a bifurcated reporting structure with you, the Summer Program Director, also reporting to one of the Division Directors as a teacher—it may be a transitional step to a more unitary structure.)

Note: While the position is noted as "academic," almost certainly (even if only at the younger ages) there still will be significant summer program elements existing, i.e., fun and games.

Given the significance of Semester 3 as an integrated part of the academic program, and given that this person is now a Division Director peer, it's clear the reporting structure must be the same as for the Division Directors. Whether that's to the School Head, the Assistant Head for Academics, or some other position, the Division Heads and the Third Semester Director must align, collaborate, and agree. Their relationship must be collegial in power as well as relationship. Currently, Summer Program Directors tend to be transitional positions, with the incumbent rarely staying for more than two or three years. For success, this position requires the kind of longevity that Division Directors evidence. Develop your leadership structure to be seen as a powerful career move, like any other administrative position.

Facilities

The relationship of program to the Business Office is important. Cramming program into 12 months of the school year, without a clearly articulated system for managing facilities (indoor and outdoor), results in chaos over time. Clearly, when the school is used year-round, it is imperative to align the academic and the building calendars. Instead of the summer being seen as the time when all major work is done, those tasks must now be spread throughout the year. Academic administrators must understand the importance of planning and the relative decrease in flexibility. Then maintenance plans can go ahead as scheduled and not be derailed by changes in the calendar. We recommend at least two planning sessions a year between the Business Office and the Division Directors to align calendars, identify issues, and develop solutions. This may also have implications for strategic planning and strategic financial planning. Yearlong programming may require, for example, investment in durable products to minimize maintenance, such as, for example, using artificial turf instead of grass playing surfaces.

Upper School

In the upper school, planning the summer program as the third semester provides a way to develop the curriculum more profoundly. Your summer program offers an opportunity for your school to reimagine mission delivery for these students. Not constrained by calendar, upper schools can offer students curricular flexibility and programmatic depth and breadth. We recommend the following.

- Schools reduce prescriptive curriculum requirements, including:
  - determining total credits required for graduation;
  - limiting curriculum requirements to, for example, four credits of English and mathematics (and religion in faith-based schools); and
  - encouraging students to follow their passions and interests by creating a program that allows for imbalance, e.g., doubling or tripling up in a subject.
- Schools develop mission-based profiles reflecting their curricular disctinctions.
  - Today, school profiles differ little school to school. With S3, schools will write profiles that clearly distinguish them from their competitors.
  - Students develop programming over their four years of upper school that clearly distinguishes them from one another, since there will now be diverse paths to graduation.
  - College counseling departments will be proactive in ensuring students who want a particular postsecondary path know and fulfill the requirements and communicating to universities and colleges the edge their students have.

Semester 3 offers an opportunity for:

- truly innovative curriculum;
- exciting pathways for students to develop themselves (and make themselves attractive to next-level college and employers);
- another genuine option for career advancement; and
- a way for schools to "force" themselves to think creatively—who they are and what they are doing.

The Summer Program Director, with the School Head's support, can lead this change and position your school as a leader in the industry and a competitor in the marketplace.

Child Safety and Risk Management

Summer is the season of exploration. But it's also one of the most dangerous times of the year for youth. Swimming accidents, outdoor mishaps, and playground bullies are all concerns for parents and summer program personnel as the season rolls toward the new school year.

Insurance Requirements and Risk Management

Schools are adding new summer programs and expanding their existing offerings as they experience the benefits to their bottom line, staff retention, and recruitment efforts. These programs bring in more dollars; can provide summer work for school employees; and, when open to the wider community, bring the school to the attention of prospective families.

However, summer programs can also bring various expanded and new risks into the picture. It's essential to reduce those risks through effective planning and training, as well as through "transferring" portions of the risk through insurance programs.

Spot the Risks in Your Summer Program

Risk management is a major concern for school leaders. It's clearer every day that, indeed, "it can happen here." Of course, your school has procedures in place designed to reduce risk—from employment policies to crisis plans to insurance coverage.

However, as Summer Program Director, you may not have looked at risk management specifically from the perspective of your program. It's one of those items that's easy to miss as you focus on putting the program together, setting the budget, hiring instructors, creating the brochure and advertising, and handling so many other tasks.

Here's a quick guide to get you thinking about the questions to ask so you can get the answers you need. Add to the list as you consider these areas based on your specific program. Then schedule a conversation with your school's Business Manager or Risk Manager to discuss any areas that are unclear or need work.

Question No. 1: Are your facilities safe?

- Have you and the Business Manager or Facilities Director done a "walk-around" check of the campus and all facilities (for example, buildings, playing fields, playgrounds, and equipment) to be used?
- Are all fire prevention, electrical, and alarm systems in good working order?
- Is the campus secure (e.g., fencing, locked gates, security)?
- Do you have a special badge or other means of visually identifying the adults involved with your program? Are guests required to have a "visitor" badge? Is a process in place for dealing with any unidentified adult?

Question No. 2: Are you prepared to handle emergencies?

- What is the process for dealing with a medical emergency—illness or injury involving a student or employee?
- Is a nurse on duty during your summer program?
- Are staff members trained in CPR and first aid?
- Do chaperones on trips carry student medical permission forms?
- In the event of an emergency that requires administering immediate medical aid, is there someone on campus designated to have access to staff and student medical records?

- Can summer program personnel easily communicate with one another (e.g., by cell phone or walkie-talkie)?
- Does your school have crisis plans covering events such as evacuation, fire, an intruder, and terrorism? Was the summer program included when these plans were created, or do they need to be modified or expanded to cover these activities?
- Who is in charge of putting the plan into action during the summer program? Who has been assigned specific duties? Who are the backups for each position?

Question No. 3: Do you review these policies, procedures, and plans during training?
- If you are not thoroughly familiar with the school's plans and policies, meet with your Business Manager and Human Resource Director to go over them.
- As you train the instructors and staff members, of course you'll need to get down to the basics with newcomers. However, do not assume that experienced staff members are up to date. Even those who have been part of the school and the summer program for years benefit from a "refresher course."

Question No. 4: What about insurance?
- Do you know what is and is not covered under each of the school's insurance policies as they relate to the summer program? Review all relevant activities and personnel with your insurance agent.
- Are you offering activities outside your school's academic-year programs—perhaps orienteering on the school grounds, wilderness-type trips, or foreign travel?
- Are you using equipment the school does not own or normally access?
- Are you taking students to an off-campus facility (YMCA, swimming pool, park)?
- What transportation options are you using?
- Does your school's liability insurance cover your instructors and staff members? What about volunteers?
- Have you performed your due diligence on the instructors' qualifications? For example, are all coaches properly licensed, and do they have CPR, AED, and first aid training?

Question No. 5: Do you have policies for employees?
- What does your contract cover for summer program employees?
- Do you require background checks?
- Do you require health screenings?
- Do you have policies on sexual harassment, drug and alcohol use, attendance, and discipline?

Even though the summertime atmosphere may be more informal, these issues are serious—and just as risky.

Question No. 6: Do you have policies for volunteers?
- Have they read and signed your "Bill of Volunteer Rights and Responsibilities"?
- Do you perform background checks?
- Do you have a protocol that prohibits any adult being "one-on-one" with a student?
- Are volunteers covered under Workers' Compensation?
- Does your liability insurance cover them?
- If they will be driving:
  – Are their operator's licenses, tags, and insurance current?
  – Does the school's automobile policy cover them?
  – Are the vehicles they operate safe and in good repair?
  – Do you require motor vehicle records checks?

Question No. 7: What about student-related matters?
- What are the logistics for drop-off and pickup?
- What happens when a student:
  – arrives late;
  – does not show up as expected for a class or activity, or
  – is not picked up at day's end?
- Can you locate a student at any time if a parent calls? How?
- Are you aware of any legal custodial issues, for example, who is and is not permitted pick to up the child?
- Do you have policies on behavior, such as bullying, drug and alcohol use, and sexual harassment?

As the Summer Program Director, you are responsible (and liable!) for your entire program. Do not leave these matters to chance.

Your goal is to ensure that you ask the important questions and get the answers. Many of these areas may be covered in current school protocols—such as background checks for all employees and emergency drills. However, you want to consider these questions as they pertain to your summer program. Then you can feel confident that you have fulfilled your responsibility to the students, their families, the school, and yourself.

When you talk with your Business Manager about these matters, don't be surprised if he or she tells you not to worry about it—it's all taken care of. Ask anyway, politely yet firmly, and don't be put off until you get the information you need. This process may strengthen your relationship with the Business Manager, who realizes that you are a valuable partner, one who takes an interest in the matters that occupy his or her mind.

Handling Monetary Issues

Summer programs give children valuable experience, bring prospective students on campus, provide summer jobs for teachers, make the campus an attraction during the summer vacation ... and are an excellent source of added revenue. Of course, the work and investment required to develop and maintain your summer program bring many benefits that cannot be measured.

Do you, however, know how much money the program has earned for the school?

Summer programs can be an excellent source of revenue, but they can also contain various "hidden" expenses. Take another look and ensure that you are calculating the full cost of operating your summer program. Only then can you allocate expenses accurately and generate a clear financial picture for both school year and summer. And because this auxiliary program should be, at minimum, self-supporting, you need to take all expenses into account to set appropriate fees.

If expenses exceed revenues, you are probably using tuition dollars to subsidize summer program costs. Not only is this unsound financial practice, but it robs current students of funds that should be devoted to their education, particularly if only a small percentage of them are enrolled in the summer program.

Set your goals for your summer program—a revenue producing and marketing vehicle—and carefully determine the costs involved in providing the classes and activities. Then you can structure your tuition and fees so they support a quality program—and one that pays its own way.

To start, research the local market's summer programs—for example, other private school programs, church programs, the YMCA—and determine their costs. To attract families, your prices should be competitive.

With that in mind, calculate a projected profit for each class based on assumed enrollment and all anticipated expenses. Once you make these calculations, you can then set a fair price for each class, a price that provides a profit margin.

Let's consider a typical one-week science program for fourth- and fifth-graders that takes place in your middle school science lab. You've limited the program to 15 students.

Expenses	
Teacher:	$700
Assistant:	$200
Expenses:	$100
Extraordinary Expenses:	$800
Subtotal:	$1,800
Profit:	**$350**
Total:	$2,150
Participant Cost: ($2,150 ÷ 15)	$143.33

Estimate your projected expenses to make sure your summer program doesn't run into the red. Calculating a reasonable profit margin can usually help mitigate any unforeseen budgetary problems.

Determining Your Projected Expenses

To determine your bottom line, you and your school's Business Manager should create a line-item budget to track all costs. Review the following to verify that all expenses appropriate to your program have been accounted for and deducted from the overall receipts, including:

- wear and tear on school-owned equipment (budgeted depreciation);
- cost of repair and replacement of school-owned items such as vans and audiovisual and laboratory equipment;
- prorated cost of service contracts on school-owned equipment shared with the summer program;
- cost of equipment purchased by the summer program then transferred to school ownership;
- setup and takedown of the summer program (such as moving desks and other supplies and equipment);
- maintenance and repair during the summer program, including work done to keep the program running smoothly;
- added costs of regular summer maintenance caused by the summer program (for example, having work performed by outside contractors because of time limits for completing routine maintenance; having maintenance people work overtime to finish projects);
- more personnel required to meet the needs of the summer program and routine maintenance;
- extra expense of custodial supplies;
- added expenses for custodian's regular duties during the summer program (for example, toilets may need daily cleaning);
- custodial and maintenance personnel costs (direct and prorated for those people who administer the summer program as part of their school contracts);
- portion of the director's salary for summer program;
- prorated costs of any other employee who works part-time for the summer program during school year (secretary, publications designer, admission person who interviews prospective summer school students, Business Office employees);
- any full-time employees of the summer program;

- direct utility costs attributed to the program (e.g., cost of making ice in the hockey rink, air-conditioning the field house, or lighting the plant for evening programs);
- indirect cost of utilities (electric, gas, or oil) to heat, cool, or ventilate, prorated by time, student population, or other method. (What would you normally spend, and what is the added summer program expense?);
- added expense for property and casualty or liability insurance attributable to summer program;
- summer program student accident insurance; and
- cost of marketing and mailing, including postage.

Without this accounting level, you may be blind to the real cost, and therefore to the real financial value of your summer program. And, as you begin thinking about next year's summer program, make sure that you have:

- tuitions and fees based on actual cost;
- a stand-alone, line-item budget designed by the Business Office and jointly administered by you and the Business Manager;
- regular sharing of the budget with the Finance Committee, even if the school budget includes only the revenue and expense totals as line items; and
- written policies for staff salaries and benefits, collection of tuition and fees, refunds, discounts, and disbursement of funds.

As a result, next year's computations should be much easier.

Summer Program Budget Example

Income

Program	Enrollment	Tuition	Total Tuition
Program	22	350	7,700
Program	30	350	10,500
Program	450	450	202,500
Program	8	500	4,000
Program	7	350	2,450
Program	19	350	6,650

Program	24	350	8,400
Program	24	350	8,400
Program	17	350	5,950

Financial Aid			-25,000
Other			350
Donations			25,000
Food			39,000
Extended Care			45,000
Store			6,530
Outside Contractor			2,200

Total Income	**349,630**

Expenses	
Expense Item	**Total Expense**
Salaries (excluding your salary)	158,000
Food	39,000
Extended Care	35,000
Store	1,580
Marketing	22,500
Transportation	9,000
Equipment (items above $100)	1,700
Materials (teaching)	3,500
Field Trips	14,500
Office Supplies	250

Postage	300
Telephone	240
Insurance	1,500
Custodial	4,100
Travel	500
Professional Development	750
Utilities	1,000

Total Expenses	**293,420**

Net Revenue	**56,210**

To next year's float	25,000
To operating	31,210

To develop a financial history for your summer program and better track its success, replicate the budget chart year-to-year to determine where you can decrease expenses and increase income. Streamlining your program becomes easier each year as you analyze your budget and make proper adjustments.

Thinking About Discounts

Most summer programs have discounting that occurs even without you knowing it's happening. This directly impacts your bottom line. And, since it might even be out of your control (i.e., school policy), you must ponder and track all those discounts. For the following discounts, write in the details of each and then consider whether they make sense, and from whose viewpoint. You may also be impacted by the views and experiences of your colleagues.

Summer Program Discounts

Staff members working in the summer program

Discount parameters:

Your thoughts about them:

School employees not working in the summer program

Discount parameters:

Your thoughts about them:

Early registration, referral, and sibling

Discount parameters:

Your thoughts about them:

Multiweek participants

Discount parameters:

Your thoughts about them:

Other

Discount parameters:

Your thoughts about them:

Financial Aid

Financial aid (tuition assistance) can also be a thorny issue. Provide it or not? If you do provide it, under what circumstances? How will you address it in the budget?

ISM does not recommend providing financial aid for your summer program. There are exceptions that may apply to your school, and that may or may not be a good idea.

1. Some schools seek donations to cover a "free" summer program seat for a child who cannot otherwise afford it. ISM has seen this at silent auctions, as Christmas "presents," and as solicited gifts. This approach must go through the Development Office to ensure the school follows protocols and treats donors respectfully (for example, not asked from different sides for diverse causes).

2. Some schools have treated summer program as they have the tuition during the year. For example, if a student received a 10% tuition discount during the school year, the same discount applies to summer program fees. This is a simple mechanism, but such automatic financial aid can cut deeply into your own budget. It is key in this scenario that you are credited for the full fee and the school absorbs the financial aid payment.

3. Another identifiable group includes students who receive free or reduced lunch. For schools with a mission to serve a wide socioeconomic range, this provides a clear indicator of need and can be addressed through clear policy and procedure.

You, as Summer Program Director, must not be involved in financial aid. If it is provided, the mechanism should be straightforward and administered by and through the Business Office. The intricacies of financial aid are many, and it is far too complicated for you to administer.

Handling Monetary Issues

Marketing and Promotion

As the Summer Program Director, you want to attract as many participants as you can to your school's summer program. Because it does not have admission requirements (except those courses that offer credit), it is often oriented toward enrichment rather than academics. The program is open to almost any student interested in a rewarding summer adventure. You can accommodate as many students as space allows.

Research Your Competition

There are surely other summer programs in your area, some that may be community stalwarts. Is your market niche unique enough to compete? What makes your program stand out from the others? To determine this, you need first to do some research.

The Competition	
School Name:	
Website:	
Academic	**Specialty/Niche**
Sports	**Performance**
Leadership	**Trips**

Internal Marketing Strategies

A challenge you face is keeping your program in the minds of the students and their families throughout the academic year. This problem is exacerbated by having participants who may have been in the summer program for only a week or two. Another challenge is that some participants may not be students at your school during the academic year and you only see them a few weeks in the summer.

Yet, these experienced participants are the prime potential students for the coming summer. Each is an excellent target for internal marketing. They have been part of the summer program for one or more years, have enjoyed themselves, and need less "selling" about the virtues and benefits of the program than those who have never attended.

Consider these marketing ideas.

- Put several articles in your school's newsletter (print and electronic) each year. Schedule one article in the early fall, used as wrap-up for the just-completed program and extolling the activities the students enjoyed. Plan for a second in the late fall or early winter, focusing on several of the new programs for the coming summer. This should appear a few weeks before opening the registration period. Use a third article as a summary of the statistics about the coming program, detailing how many students are registered, introducing the teachers who will be involved, and advertising any underenrolled activities.

- Make sure the summer program pages on your school's website are up to date with fresh material. Before finalizing the offerings, post the dates of the program and when registration begins. Once you determine the offerings, post that information immediately. Send a blast email invitation to all of last summer's participants, and provide a direct link to the summer program webpage. Send another email, with a link to the web section, when registration opens.

- Post signs around campus with the dates of the program. As the academic year progresses, change the signs to highlight some of the new offerings.

- Several times a year, ask for time to meet with the faculty. Use this time to recruit new teachers and ask for ideas for activities. Discuss past programs' successes. ("Last summer we had 327 participants, 278 from our school. This fall we enrolled 37 new students who were introduced to our school through the summer program.") Give the teachers fliers about the program to distribute among their students.

- Speak at student assemblies. Describe the exciting courses your summer program offers. Ask several teachers and past participants to speak, as well.

- Set up booths at open houses and home athletics contests. Have information about the coming summer's program available. Invite several teachers who will lead the activities, plus some former student participants, and have them wear summer program T-shirts.

- If your school conducts an auction during the school year, donate a free week for a participant. This not only raises money for the school, but highlights the summer program.

- When a new student enrolls in your school, send the family information about the summer program and, if the time is appropriate, registration materials.
- During the winter holidays, send a card to last summer's attendees to remind them of the fun they had during the summer. Picture one of the events or a group of last year's teachers. Send out a refrigerator magnet showing the calendar. Also, during the holidays, have a reunion for previous participants to rekindle interest in the coming summer. Ask teachers for the coming program to be there as well.
- During the academic year, publish a summer program newsletter with editions sent to past participants.

Marketing your summer program to past participants generates interest for the coming summer in an audience already predisposed to return. These students are the most likely to register again. Enhance that possibility by making sure you have sufficiently and effectively informed and encouraged them.

Use the following template to help you focus your efforts.

Whom am I influencing?	
Potential strategies?	

Internal Marketing Strategies	Cost

External Marketing Strategies

Your external marketing targets are families who have not enrolled students in your summer program in the last two years—even if the students are enrolled in your school during the academic year.

Advertisements: For several weeks before opening summer program registration, advertise in local newspapers and magazines. Ask the Admission Office where it advertises the school's open houses and testing dates. See if that office is planning to run any advertisements at the same times as you, the Summer Program Director, are planning yours. If so, explore the possibility of combining efforts with some advertisements highlighting the admission activity with a small mention of the summer program and (vice versa).

Check with the local newspapers to see if they have special "summer camp" issues in which you can advertise. Your summer program's presence will be mandatory in that edition (and may be more noticed in a negative way if it is absent).

Advertising fills a special niche in marketing your summer program. No advertisement, without other stimuli, will "sell" a family and cause them to enroll. Consider advertising as a way to let people know your school has a summer program and a means of conveying ways to obtain more information.

Direct Mail: Develop a direct-mail piece that concisely describes your program, giving contact and website information. Besides mailing the piece to prospective families, print extra copies to use in other effective ways. Ask the Admission Office to include the piece in every response to an inquiry. If you hire outside specialist instructors (for example, ballet, karate, swimming), give them copies to distribute to their students. (These specialists can also be a good external advertising medium. Ask them to share their mailing lists so you can expand your database.) Ask doctors, pediatricians, orthodontists, etc., to place copies of the piece in their waiting rooms. Any time there is an outside group on campus, have pieces available. Provide the piece to all relocation offices in the area. (Check with the Admission Office to see which ones they are in contact with.)

Direct mail offers you another opportunity to "get your name out there." Create your message around one central, compelling aspect of the summer program (i.e., something unique your program offers). See a direct-mail piece, no matter how it is used, as a way to give readers a taste of your summer program and leave them with a hunger for more information.

Brochure: Send copies of the summer program brochure to all current families (those with students enrolled in the academic year program and those whose children attended last summer's program). Or send an email with a link to the brochure PDF on the website. Ask the Admission Office to include the brochure in all acceptance letters. Provide copies of the brochure to all feeder schools. (Again, the Admission Office can identify for you which feeder schools have been propitious for them.)

Give several copies of the brochure to competing programs. There will be some overlap in offerings, but you should have several courses that only your program provides. Having your program's brochure makes it easy for those directors to assist families seeking a specific offering. Also, provide copies of the brochure to schools that do not have a summer program.

The brochure—in print and on the school's website—is your chief marketing piece. Fill it with the most compelling information about the program.

Besides a complete listing of all the offerings, dates, and registration information, the brochure should demonstrate why a family should enroll their child in your school's summer program. Include pictures with captions of activities from the previous year. ("Students in the technology class build their own computer.")

Add statistics that show growth. ("The 16 students who enrolled in the SAT prep class experienced an average increase in their total score of 28 points.")

Validating quotations from the previous year's participants and parents are effective testimonials. ("When Jonny was enrolled in the I&P Academy Summer Program, he was up each day eager to go. We did not have that experience the year before when he was attending another summer program.")

Make sure to include the benefits the students will enjoy for attending the summer program. ("In this water safety class you will be certified to be a lifeguard, and learn first aid and CPR.")

Meetings: Ask several parents whose students participated in last year's summer program to host living room coffees for potential families. If the Admission Office holds these gatherings, ask to attend and distribute the direct-mail piece. Have a booth at a camp fair, if there is one in your area.

For each public event on your campus (for example, home athletics contests, back-to-school nights, open houses, drama and music performances, parenting education events) set up a booth with information about the summer program. Besides having the direct-mail piece available, have examples of any "giveaways" that you provided last summer—for example, T-shirts and lanyards.

Electronic: Make sure the summer program has an evident presence on your school's website—including a page of its own that is readily identifiable (i.e., not "buried" in a drop-down menu for another school program). Given the profound, positive effect the summer program can have on the school's finances, enrollment, and image, a prominent place on the website is mandatory.

Several times a year, send an email to current parents (in your school for the academic year and parents of students who attended last summer's program and are not in your school). In the email, include links to the summer program webpage(s) and a PDF download of the program's brochure. Ask these parents to send the email to families they know that have children who would benefit from attending your summer program.

Miscellaneous: Place signs on the perimeter of the campus (if local zoning regulations allow). Put posters in the local libraries, with some of the direct-mail pieces. These should contain the program's dates and contact information.

Summary: Marketing your summer program to families that have not used your services is key to increasing your summer program's enrollment. Internal marketing yields more dividends because you are marketing to families already familiar with the program. Plus, your summer program (and therefore your school) benefits from attracting families currently unfamiliar with the service you provide.

Use the following template to help you focus your efforts.

Whom am I influencing?	
Potential strategies?	

External Marketing Strategies	Cost

Once you've determined your external marketing strategies, review how they impact your online presence—particularly in how your website is structured and appeals to potential participants for your summer program. Today, this emphasis is critical to the success of your inbound marketing. With this in mind, consider the following questionnaire.

Inbound Marketing Questionnaire	
1. Pretend you are a prospective parent looking for a school in your area and conduct an online search (e.g., Google, Yahoo). Where do you rank in organic results? How do your competitors rank?	
2. Review two or three of your school's summer program website pages.	
Is your site primarily geared to prospective families?	Y N
Is your navigation structure intuitive?	Y N
Are you "writing for the web"?	Y N
Is your content rich with applicable keywords?	Y N
Are you properly using: Page titles? Headers? Meta descriptions?	 Y N Y N Y N

Get Your Money's Worth From Summer Program Advertisements

What's on your list of strategies for promoting your summer program? You've probably put together a brochure to distribute to current families, inquiries, people who came to the open houses, and, if you have a program, to families in your "draw" areas. You might also use posters and banners, a notice on the school sign, and articles in your newsletters.

For most schools, advertising also ranks high on the list. Following a few simple guidelines can help ensure that you get the most for every dollar you spend. And while this section focuses on print advertisements, many of the same principles can be applied to radio spots as well.

The Technical Side
Budget: There is no hard-and-fast rule for determining a "reasonable" amount to spend on advertising. One sensible approach is to base your budget on your fees.

Say, for example, that you charge $175 a week for your "Swim and Sun" program and expect to attract 600 children over the course of the summer. How many weekly fees will you invest in advertising?

Remember that a series of three advertisements in each of three carefully selected publications has much greater impact than single ads in 10 different spots. And it can be more economical, too. (See "Where to advertise" below.)

Timing: To get the most from your advertising, you need to know when families you want to attract start making their summer plans. If you offer a day program and recruit from the local area, is April too soon? Not soon enough? Is it worthwhile to run ads in late May or early June to pick up those last-minute decision-makers?

If you have a boarding program and decide to advertise in regional and national magazines, you need to plan farther ahead to meet those deadlines.

Where to advertise: For the best balance of visibility and price, you may find that weekly community newspapers give you the most for your money. Schools also report that free parent-oriented publications (usually found on grocery store display racks) have worked for them. Again, you need to know the families you target, when they're making choices, and what they're reading—newspapers, magazines, free publications (delivered and off the rack).

Some schools have advertised successfully in the "school and camp" sections in national and regional publications (such as *Boys' Life Magazine, The Wall Street Journal,* and *Southern Living*). Or match your ads directly with readers' interests through various specialty publications. Feature your summer arts program in the playbill for the local theater, for example, or your sports camp in the golf course's newsletter.

Keep an eye out for the best deals for placement and price. An ad in a special summer camp section or a spot on the sports page—which is most effective for the program you run?

Talk with an advertising representative about getting the best position and price. For example, if you're dealing with a chain of local newspapers, you can stretch your dollar. You pay the basic rate in the highest-priced paper, then a reduced "pickup" rate when you place the same ad in one or more of the other papers in the group.

Standing Out From the Crowd

A "typical" summer program advertisement often reads like this:

> **Summer at XYZ Academy**
>
> June 3–July 26, 2018
> Academics, recreation, arts & crafts
> Age 3–Grade 12
>
> **XYZ Academy**
> 200 Academy Road
> Schoolville   111-234-5678

As the parent of a nine-year-old girl, the basic information you need is there. The program fits your daughter's age and her interest in arts and crafts. The school is within reasonable driving distance and the timing is right—you leave for vacation in late July.

Then you look at the advertisement right below it.

> *Academics—catch up or move ahead*
> *The arts—from finger painting to pottery*
> *Recreation—lacrosse, hiking, and much more*
>
> **Join us for summer fun
> at I&P Academy!**
>
> June 3–July 26, 2018
>
> More than 30 classes and activities
> for boys and girls age 3–Grade 12
>
> For a brochure, call
> Sylvia Verano, Program Director,
> at 111-222-3456.
>
> **I&P Academy**
> 400 Country Road, Schoolville

Same age group, same basic program, same dates, nearby location—but this ad gives you a stronger idea of the breadth of the arts-and-crafts offerings and the quality of the program overall. It's more informative, it's more personal, and it encourages you to take action. You might call both schools for information, but which has made the strongest first impression?

If you place your advertisement in a special summer program section, keep in mind that you'll be in competition for the reader's attention. Your ad must be either large enough or distinctive enough—preferably both—to stand out on the page.

Combine concise, well-thought-out copy with a photograph of excited, involved kids, a quotation from a parent or child, and a clean, easy-to-read layout, and you'll have an advertisement that gets noticed. Remember that besides promoting your summer activities, it's also important for your ad to reflect the quality of your program and your school.

Use Your Ads
Once you've created effective summer program ads, get the most out of them. Run them in your school newsletter. Print them up as oversized postcards—an effective, economical way to spread the word to potential summer campers, day or boarding. Or turn them into posters to display in store windows.

Keeping Track of Your Success
"I saw your ad in the Post." "I heard about you on the radio." "I got your brochure in the mail." "The neighbors say your program is great." These are the comments you want to collect and then review as part of your summer program wrap-up.

When parents call for information, have the receptionist ask, "How did you hear about us?" Create a simple form—with a space for the date and a checklist of your promotional efforts—to keep by the phone.

Once you know what works, making those basic decisions on what to do, when to do it, and how much to spend are a snap.

Review Your Online Presence

No discussion of marketing today can exclude the power of the internet and your school's online presence. It is likely that parents looking for summer programs for their children turn to the internet first—and, if your program does not show up in their search, you're virtually invisible.

Of course, host your summer program on your school website. Or it can have its own dedicated site. There are advantages (and disadvantages) to either approach. Consider the families you hope to attract. If primarily current parents and students at your school, having the program on the school website makes sense. But, if you want to throw a "wider net," a dedicated site may be a better choice. You can also do both!

As you review your online presence, consider the following elements to "kickstart" your thinking. Expand these if you like. Add more. This is meant to be a template to start your analysis.

Your Summer Program's Online Presence
Search Optimization   List three ways you can improve your search engine results.
1.   2.   3.
Website   List three ways you can improve your website presence (one short-term, two long-term).
1.   2.   3.
Content   List two ways you can improve your inbound marketing content (one short-term, one long-term).
1.   2.
Landing Page   List one way you can improve your "request for information" page.
1.
Social Media   List two ways you can improve your social media strategy and content (two short-term).
1.   2.

Summer Program as a Recruitment Strategy

As the Summer Program Director, you are aware that many (if not most) of your summer program participants attend other schools in your area, including public schools. These are potential students for your private school, and you would like them to consider applying. However, you worry about your school's image. You do not want to appear to "take advantage" of this special situation where the students are daily on your campus. Here are subtle strategies to better educate these students and their families about your school.

- When a student from another school enrolls in the summer program, ask the Admission Office to send the family a copy of your school's recruitment materials. In a personal cover letter, explain that all noncurrent families receive these materials to help them understand the excellence they can expect at your school, in the school-year and summer programs.

- When the summer program begins, display examples of student work from the just-completed academic year. These displays should clearly demonstrate the breadth and quality of your school's programs.

- At the end of the summer program, give everyone who has attended a certificate. Make sure that your school's name and logo stand out. This provides students with a tangible reminder of their participation in your summer program.

- Throughout the program and in all your literature, identify schoolteachers who work in the summer program. Parents are attracted as much to the people who teach their children as they are to a school's educational offerings.

- Once students have attended the summer program, have the Admission Office put the families on the mailing list to receive the school newsletter during the academic year. The School Head can write a cover letter explaining that the school wants to keep them abreast of other events in the life of the school.

- During the next academic year, invite the summer program students and their families to all admission open houses. If there are enough students from other schools entering the summer program, consider holding a special open house just for those families.

- If current families hold admission-oriented "coffees" in their homes, invite families from the summer program to attend. They hear about the school in an effective way and meet satisfied parents—your best marketers.

- Publish a summer program newsletter. Show how the quality of your summer program is an example of the excellence of the academic-year program. Send a wrap-up edition of the newsletter in the fall to remind those in other schools of the exciting time they had last summer.

- During the academic year, hold a summer program reunion to bring nonschool participants back on campus. It is a good way to reinforce the friendships and excitement from the previous summer and associate them with your school. If you hold the reunion around the time you send registration materials for the coming summer, you perform double duty—recruiting for both the academic year and the summer.

- Consider having programs designed for students younger than your school's youngest students. For example, if your school begins with seventh grade, create a program that serves elementary grade students. As students reach the top grade of their present school and consider options for the next year, your school might be the one they choose.

No matter how effectively you implement any of these strategies, there can be no substitute for a student having a good experience in your school's summer program. Part of this experience will be the personal connection these students and their families develop with your school. As you put strategies in place, remember that it takes time for them to be successful—success being defined as summer program students applying for the academic-year program. Many students will not apply immediately and may wait a year or two. So, you should track academic-year applicants from all summer programs, not just the most recent.

Recruiting Home-Schoolers

You're likely to enroll public school students in your summer program. But don't ignore an often overlooked group of students—home-schoolers.

Judging from its incredible growth in the past two decades, home-schooling has clearly become more acceptable for parents seeking alternative education for their children. Like charter schools, home-schooling groups can be perceived as competition for private schools. However, it may be more advantageous to cooperate with home-schoolers than to compete with them. Although students of all ages are educated at home, many are younger children who eventually attend conventional schools. Home-schooling parents typically have views on education that mirror those held by your school's parents, and their children often prove to be exemplary private school students. With this in mind, consider working with local home-schooling groups as you would collaborate with feeder schools.

Home-schooling parents often desire help, which is often provided through parent networks and home-schooling organizations. Your private school can offer many resources these families need—in a way that meets the "mission" of their home education and builds a relationship with them. Inviting home-schoolers to attend your summer program, in particular, is one way to bring these students "into the fold."

With some research, you're likely to find parent networks nearby. Contact your state Department of Education for a listing of any organized home-school groups in your area. Publicize your openness to work with home educators. When advertising your summer program, for example, mention that "home-schoolers are welcome."

Place interested home-schooling families on your mailing list to receive newsletters, fliers for upcoming social events, and other marketing materials. You may want to invite candidates to appropriate school events like concerts, plays, and special sports competitions. In short, welcome them to your "family."

As with any recruitment tactic, the key is to get the potential student on your campus. Your summer program is a perfect opportunity to show home-schoolers the services and culture your school provides, as they get to know many of your students, faculty, and staff members. If it is a pleasant, fulfilling experience, students will want to attend full-time—and their parents may oblige.

Assessing Your Program and Preparing for Next Year

The summer is over and the new school year is soon to begin (for year-round schools, the fall session is already in gear). Another summer program is in the bag. Now is the time to revisit and reassess what you offered, who attended, and the strength of your bottom line. By setting goals now for next summer, you can take your summer program to the next level to recruit and re-recruit students and enhance your hard income. Ideally, as your program evolves over the years, the planning becomes cyclical, as shown in the following diagram.

Quality Improvement Cycle

PLAN
Set Program improvement goals and develop and implement a plan for achieving them

TRAIN
Develop staff understanding and ownership of program quality goals and strategies

ASSESS
Look for evidence of quality improvement during the program

REFLECT
Review summer program data and debrief witrh key stakeholders

Evaluating Your Current Program

Consider your just completed program. What worked? What didn't work? What hole in the program might you need to fill? What new opportunities are emerging?

As Summer Program Director, here are a few basic strategies to help you boost your program:

- Evaluate your most recent program, facilities, staff, and equipment soon after summer, while the experience is still fresh.
- Review comments collected from students, parents, and staff members. If there was no "exit" evaluation conducted, conduct an informal or formal survey to collect essential feedback.

- Check out the competition—see what is not available and would fit well in your community, and look for ways your program can meet families' needs.
- Review your marketing materials and plan improvements if needed.
- Look for other community facilities that would help you fulfill your mission if your campus cannot support the program.

How to Assess Teacher Impact in Your Summer Program

Knowing how effective your summer program teachers are is essential in maintaining and improving the reputation of your program, and thus your ability to sustain or increase its size. The reputation of your summer program is almost entirely dependent on the impact that faculty have on students for the brief time they teach and entertain them, typically in one-week periods. The school's reputation is always at stake, particularly if most attendees are not the school's regular students. The Summer Program Director must have a way to evaluate faculty and encourage teachers to return in subsequent years (if skilled) or denied that opportunity (if ineffective).

Here the next obstacle arises. During the school year, teachers have an extended period of time to:

– really get to know the students;

– design a clearly focused curriculum with support structures (collegial and administrative); and

– develop a sequence of activities which, over time, can be expected to engage students.

In the summer, teachers often work independently, with perhaps limited administrative support. They must connect with students and engage them, perhaps only a week at a time. They are expected to be entertainers as well as educators. Clearly, the summer program objectives require a different set of skills.

The term "evaluating impact" of summer program teachers is used in preference to evaluation or assessment. The likelihood that a student returns the next year is contingent on aspects that would have far less relevance in the regular school year.

Consider using the following strategies.

Strategy No. 1

Survey the parents of participants at the end of each session or course offering. (Do this on paper or electronically, depending on the circumstances of your program. Personalize with the course title, date, and name of the instructor.)

Summer Program Survey: Parent
Please respond to the following statements by circling a number (5 is fully accurate; 1 is not accurate at all). In the space at the bottom, we welcome any comments that you might have. Thank you.
Session/course offering: _____ **Date:** _____   **Name of teacher(s)** _____
1. My child looked forward to arriving at summer program every day.   1   2   3   4   5
2. My child had a program that conforms to the school's high standards.   1   2   3   4   5
3. My child really enjoyed the instructor(s).   1   2   3   4   5
4. We found the program/camp to be safe.   1   2   3   4   5
5. As a parent, I was pleased with the communication I received from the summer program.   1   2   3   4   5
6. This year's summer program met or exceeded my expectations.   1   2   3   4   5
7. I will probably enroll my child in next year's summer program.   YES   NO
Comments (commendations for teachers, ways for us to improve, etc.):

Scoring and Use of the Parent Survey

1. Break down the responses, item by item, into percentages.
2. Sum the percent responses at the "good" end of the five-point scale. For example, 33% (4s) plus 17% (5s), equals 50%.
3. Follow the same procedure with the first six items. Count item number seven as 100% or 0%.
4. Collate results by individual program and by entire summer program.
5. Publicize the results, and compare year-to year.

Strategy No. 2

Survey the student participants, on paper or electronically, before they leave at the end of each session. Schedule time on the last day to complete the survey. You should fill in the camp session, date, and instructor's name.

Students in grade 4 and above can use this survey. It might be better to interview younger children and record their responses. Note: Address the need for confidentiality of written surveys by providing a sealed envelope for the student to return his or her survey response.

Summer Program Survey: Student

Please respond to the following four statements by circling a number (5 is fully accurate; 1 is not accurate at all). In the space at the bottom, we welcome any comments that you might have. Thank you.

Session/course offering: _____   **Date:** _____

Name of teacher(s) _____

1. I looked forward to arriving at the summer every day.   1   2   3   4   5
2. I knew exactly what my instructor(s) expected of me (i.e., I knew how the teacher(s) defined success).   1   2   3   4   5
3. I knew exactly what I could expect from my instructor(s) (i.e., consistency in their responses to my behaviors, academic and other).   1   2   3   4   5

4. I was treated fairly by all my instructors.   1   2   3   4   5
5. I had a lot of fun at the summer program.   1   2   3   4   5
6. This year's summer program met or exceeded my expectations.   1   2   3   4   5
7. I want to do the summer program again next year.   YES   NO
Tell us what you really liked: Tell us how we can improve what we do:

Scoring and Use of the Student Survey

1. Break down the responses, item by item, into percentages.
2. Sum the percent responses at the "good" end of the five-point scale. For example, 33% (4s) plus 17% (5s), equals 50%.
3. Follow the same procedure with the first six items. Count item number seven as 100% or 0%.
4. Collate results by individual program and by entire summer program.
5. Publicize the results, and compare year-to year.

Strategy No. 3

Carry out a survey three months after your last summer program session, to be completed by the parent and child together.

Summer Program Survey: Follow-up
Please take a minute to answer our brief survey of your experience at our 20___ summer program. Thank you. **Session/course offering:** _____ **Date:** _____ **Name of teacher(s)** _____
1. I still remember the things we did at summer camp!   1   2   3   4   5
2. I am looking forward to next summer and the information you send.   1   2   3   4   5
Please fill in topics that you would be really interested in. I wonder if you will have a summer program that …
Parents only: What would you like us to know that will help us in our planning?

How to Use Your Survey Results

As the Summer Program Director, use the survey instruments to help you decide which sessions are effective, which ones need attention, and which courses to eliminate. Also, decide what constitutes satisfactory (or not) teacher performance in the summer program. How you use the survey results in an evaluative sense is up to you. What is essential is that you use the feedback to establish criteria for strengthening your program.

Your teachers have a short time to make an impact during the summer program. Ensure that you hold them accountable for the child's experience while on your campus and under your direction. Using simple measures such as those suggested here aids you in establishing objective criteria for decision making and ensuring that your summer program enhances the reputation of your school.

"The same old classes this year!" That's the last comment you want parents and kids to make when they open your summer program brochure. Still, you know you need a balance between those successful standbys and the new offerings. With too many unfamiliar courses, you risk lowering enrollment. You may also decide to avoid classes that require too much preparation, equipment, or space, or require special skills of the instructor.

So how do you come up with strong new courses that are fun, attention-grabbing, and easy to implement? Put your creativity to work—with the help of your teachers and staff members—and develop low-maintenance classes with high kid appeal.

Looking Back by Program and Courses

With your survey results, look back at your program. Which courses are fine as-is? Which need to be strengthened? Which should be dropped and replaced? If possible, determine how courses have fared over the past few years. What works and what doesn't? It may be the course teacher and not the course content, or vice versa.

As you consider the success of your different courses and the potential for next year's program, be mindful of those that generate the most revenue. Next year, offer those classes three or four times, rather than the usual one or two. They're popular and profitable for a reason.

Use the following table as a template to track your courses year-to-year.

Course Title	Year	Enrollment	Teacher	Comments: Retain, Renew, Drop—Why?

Conclusion

Always keep in mind that a successful summer program requires a "team effort" involving you, as the Summer Program Director, and your collaboration with others on the school's Leadership Team. Keep the focus on the mission and maintain a child-centered program that caters to your families and their children.

We've given you much to ponder in this book. We hope you find it helpful as you continue to streamline and enhance your summer program!

www.ingramcontent.com/pod-product-compliance
Lightning Source LLC
Chambersburg PA
CBHW082213300426
44117CB00016B/2797